M.

Wisconsin Gas Building and Firstar Center
loom in the night's sky.

Milwaukee Architecture
A Guide to Notable Buildings

Joseph Korom

Prairie Oak Press
Madison, Wisconsin

Polished brass trim at entrance of Wells Building,
324 East Wisconsin Avenue, H. C. Koch and Company, 1901.

917.75
Kon
pb
copy

First edition, first printing
Copyright © 1995 by Joseph Korom

Prairie Oak Press
821 Prospect Place
Madison, WI 53703

Designed by Flying Fish Graphics, Blue Mounds, WI.
Printed in the United States of America by BookCrafters, Chelsea, MI.

Library of Congress Cataloging-in-Publication Data

Korom, Joseph J.
    Milwaukee architecture: a guide to notable buildings / Joseph Korom. — 1st ed.
        p. cm.
        Includes index.
        ISBN 1-879483-27-0: $18.95
        1. Architecture—Wisconsin—Milwaukee—Guidebooks. 2. Milwaukee (Wis.)—Buildings, structures, etc.—Guidebooks. 3. Milwaukee (Wis.)—Guidebooks. 4. Architects—Wisconsin—Biography.
    I. Title
NA735.M45K68 1995
720'.9775'95—dc20   95-4057
                                                     CIP

Contents

Milwaukee City Hall photograph, courtesy City of Milwaukee. All other photographs by author.

Cover photo: Dusk over Downtown Milwaukee, as viewed from Mac Arthur Square.

Back cover photo: Gilded griffin, crafted by Gould Bros. & Dibblee of Chicago. Mitchell Building, 207 East Michigan Street, Edward Townsend Mix, 1876.

Downtown Milwaukee as viewed from
Mac Arthur Square at sunset.

Germania Building, from a turn-of-the-century postcard.

Introduction

Milwaukee possesses an impressive list of architecturally significant buildings. The buildings included here, particular to their time and place, represent the values of Milwaukeeans as they were influenced by culture, technologies, and climate. Our architecture defines us, and it is our legacy to future generations.

History, events, and attitudes have shaped Milwaukee's buildings. Architects are assigned the task of translating the dreams, hopes, values, and needs of people into the stuff of the city: the brick, wood, stone, steel, and glass fabric that surrounds us. We also owe a debt to the "builders," to those carpenters, bricklayers, stonecutters, and laborers who possessed the knowledge to put a building together, yet were not formally educated. Their legacy is with us too.

Milwaukee's early days were difficult. Winters were harsh, summers were hot and humid. The early cabins were put up on whatever firm land could be found. Acres of marshes, bogs, and "impenetrable tamarack swamps" filled with cattails and mosquitos welcomed the first settlers. Three rivers, the Milwaukee, Menomonee, and Kinnickinnic, harbored abundant fish and wildlife, but often spilled over their banks. Encampments of Potawatomi, Chippewa, Ottawa, and Menominee people were nearby.

Three men, Solomon Juneau, Byron Kilbourn, and George H. Walker, share credit for founding Milwaukee. Juneau was the first to arrive.

Solomon Juneau was born on August 9, 1793, at L'Assomption Parish, near Montreal, Canada. He visited what is now downtown Milwaukee as early as September 14, 1818, as he traveled throughout Wisconsin as trader and explorer. In 1820 he settled in Milwaukee and married 15-year-old Josette Vieau (1804-1855). She was the daughter of another French Canadian, Jacques Vieau (1767-1852), who had constructed a cabin and trading post near what is now the Mitchell Park Conservatory (see building #96) as early as 1795. Vieau eventually left the area and relocated to Green Bay.

During the first five years of their marriage, Solomon and Josette Juneau resided with the Vieau family. In 1825, the Juneaus moved into the first home in what was to become the city of Milwaukee. This 12-by-16-foot structure, a combination dwelling and storeroom, was constructed with tamarack logs. Today, the high-rise 100 East Building (see building #27) occupies the site of this cabin.

In 1835, the Juneau family relocated to a more formal, two-story frame dwelling, where the Mitchell Building (see building #24) stands today. It was from this home that Juneau sold property to other early settlers and governed Milwaukee as its first mayor in 1846-1847. James S. Buck, in his *Pioneer History of Milwaukee* (1876), gives a sense of the rough-and-tumble environment in the new settlement:

> In his [Juneau's] front yard were two posts,
> about twelve feet high, to each of which a bear
> was chained; and I have spent many an hour
> in watching the gambols of those bears. They
> would climb to the top of these posts, place all
> of their feet close together, and from thence
> survey the crowd of loafers and idlers that
> were watching them, with the greatest compla-
> cency. They were killed and eaten at a feast
> Juneau gave the Indians in 1837.

Solomon Juneau died on November 14, 1856, and was buried in Calvary Cemetery. A Milwaukee street, a park, a high-rise apartment complex, and a high school are named after him.

Byron Kilbourn was an acquaintance and a rival of Juneau. Born in Granby, Connecticut, on September 8, 1801, this Yankee surveyor arrived in Milwaukee in May 1834. He claimed land, and platted and sold parcels to later arrivals. Kilbourn served two terms as Milwaukee's mayor, in 1848-1849 and again in 1853-1854. Seeking relief from rheumatism in 1868, he moved to Jacksonville, Florida, where he died on December 16, 1870. A Milwaukee street and a park are named in his honor.

George H. Walker was born in Lynchburg, Virginia, on October 22, 1811. Walker was a merchant, a trader with the Indians, and a real estate developer. He arrived in Milwaukee in the fall of 1833, wintered with Juneau, and in

1834 built a small cabin on the south bank of the Milwaukee River. His settlement, later known as Walker's Point, was located on what is now Milwaukee's near south side. Walker served two terms as mayor, from 1850 through 1853. He died on September 20, 1866 at his home on what is now East Kilbourn Avenue. A street, a city square, and a school are named for him.

The Village of Milwaukee was organized on February 27, 1837. A legislative enactment, approved March 11, 1839, consolidated the east (Juneau's) and west (Kilbourn's) wards as the Town of Milwaukee. Ownership of lands on the south side of the river (Walker's) was in dispute, but eventually the three sections were united under a single municipal government. On January 31, 1846, Milwaukee, which already had a population of some 18,000, was incorporated as a city.

As early as 1835, Milwaukee's first brickyard and sawmill were in operation. The first bricks were made in September 1835 and used in the construction of a chimney for Solomon Juneau's new wood frame house. By 1850, Milwaukee's population topped 20,000, and brick makers and masons were in demand. Businessmen preferred the permanence that brick and stone structures offered. Milwaukee came to be known as "Cream City" as factories, tanneries, breweries, warehouses, hotels, office blocks, and churches were constructed of the yellowish-white bricks that are unique to this city.

Cream City brick played a major role in the architecture of this community; no other architectural item is so inextricably tied to Milwaukee.

In his *History of Milwaukee Wisconsin* (1931), John G. Gregory noted:

> There was disappointment at first at the color
> of the bricks, when it was found that the heat
> of the kiln turned the clay to a pale yellow
> instead of red, as in the case of bricks pro-
> duced elsewhere. However, Milwaukee bricks
> proved excellent in quality, and eventually
> their color came to be esteemed as an advan-
> tage. Architects as far east as Toledo sent for
> them to use in trimming, with the view of
> securing artistic effect. When travelers praised

the cheerful appearance of structures made of Milwaukee brick, the townsfolk not only became reconciled, but learned to regard the distinctive color with local pride.

By 1849 there were nine brickyards on Milwaukee's south side, site of extensive clay deposits. Two types of Cream City bricks were produced—common and pressed. Common brick was porous and easily absorbed dirt and dust. It discolored quickly, usually as a result of the many coal furnaces belching out soot. Pressed brick was harder and stronger, and it resisted many of the discoloring elements in the atmosphere.

Milwaukee's most celebrated Cream City brick maker was George Burnham (1816-1889), an easterner from Plattsburg, New York, who moved to Milwaukee in 1843. He and his brother Jonathan opened a brickyard just south of the Menomonee River near present-day 13th Street. By 1848, the Burnham brickyard boasted 150 acres atop a stratum of clay "containing the requisite constituents of good brick." The advent of an inexpensive, steam-powered, brick-making machine assured the Burnham Brothers success. After 13 years, the brothers' partnership dissolved, although each continued to independently manufacture bricks. By 1870, George Burnham took his sons, Charles and John, into his firm, which then became known as George Burnham & Sons. Together they operated what was termed in 1881 "the world's leading brickyard." At one point the Burnhams employed 300 men and turned out some 16 million bricks annually, the majority of Cream City brick production.

Still standing on Milwaukee's near south side (907 West National Avenue) is the J. L. Burnham Block, which was the company's office headquarters. Completed in 1875, it is a three-story structure of Victorian Gothic design. The Burnham Block is the last vestige of the once famous brickyards and is, of course, constructed of Cream City brick.

The first architects who settled in Milwaukee had been trained in Germany. They interpreted their values and aesthetics recalling forms they knew well in Europe, so Milwaukee's first major buildings were Gothic, Renaissance, and Baroque-inspired. Many of Milwaukee's first crop of homegrown architects were offspring of German immigrants, which also helps explain the Teutonic appearance of Milwaukee buildings during the last half of the nineteenth century. The city skyline became a potpourri of towers, steeples, and domes. Europe was the model, and Milwaukee's architects responded accordingly.

By the time of the Civil War, Milwaukee's population topped 46,000. Ten years later it was 75,000, and by 1880 Milwaukee had 120,000 residents. As the population grew, the number of buildings increased accordingly. By the 1890s, the first skyscrapers appeared and a spectacular new City Hall towered over Milwaukee. Downtown was linked to its neighborhoods by electric trolleys and to America by its two train stations. Milwaukee businesses were leaders in publishing, tanning, brewing, banking, insurance, commodities trading, machinery manufacturing, meat packing, and shipbuilding.

Dozens of architects contributed their design skills to building Milwaukee, but the city's most noted and prolific architects were Edward Townsend Mix, Henry C. Koch, and Alexander C. Eschweiler.

Edward Townsend Mix (1831-1890) was born in New Haven, Connecticut. In 1855, he moved to Chicago, where he became an architect and business partner of William W. Boyington (1818-1898), who designed Chicago's famous Water Tower (1867). Mix arrived in Milwaukee in 1856 and by 1866 was so successful that he had a large office in the Small Block (see building #14), a commercial block that he had designed. Mix designed such Milwaukee landmarks as the Mitchell, Grain Exchange and Plankinton buildings. Although he was known for his interpretations of historical styles, he also designed one of Minneapolis's first skyscrapers, the 12-story Guaranty Loan Building (since demolished). Mix left the Cream City a rich legacy of Victorian homes, office buildings, department stores and churches.

Henry C. Koch (pronounced "cook") was born in Hanover, Germany, in 1841 and was brought to America as an infant. In August 1862, he enlisted in the Wisconsin infantry and served under General Sheridan as a topographical engineer. Upon leaving the army in 1866 Koch established his architectural practice in Milwaukee. Throughout the next four decades, Koch created some of Milwaukee's most notable buildings, including his masterpiece, the lavish City Hall. Koch's inspiration came mainly from the architectural styles of northern Europe. The domes and towers of Baroque Germany and the Low Countries held special fascination for him and are reflected in much of his work. His eldest son, Armand, became an architect and practiced with his father. Henry Koch died in 1910.

Alexander Chadbourne Eschweiler (1865-1940) and his sons Alexander, Jr. and Theodore together designed some of Milwaukee's most noteworthy buildings. The elder Eschweiler was born in Boston and moved to Milwaukee in 1882. He attended Marquette University, and studied architecture at Cornell University, graduating in 1870. The firm Eschweiler and Eschweiler was founded in 1892.

The Eschweilers were known for their adept interpretations of the English styles of the Jacobean, Elizabethan, and Tudor periods. Their designs also borrowed from the French Renaissance, and after World War I they produced buildings in the Art Deco and International styles. The firm of Eschweiler and Eschweiler was noted for the many mansions they designed for Milwaukee's elite. The firm was also responsible for a number of the campus buildings at what is now the University of Wisconsin-Milwaukee.

Acknowledgments

I wish to thank the people who assisted me in preparing this book. Judy Simonsen, Curator of Research Collections at the Milwaukee County Historical Society, helped me learn more about Milwaukee's history. Les Volmert of Milwaukee's Historic Preservation Commission shared his knowledge and answered questions for me that no one else could. Kathy Ellis of Miller Brewery, Denise Philippe of the Performing Arts Center, and John Steiner of Pabst Brewery provided information about their companies' buildings. The staffs of the Milwaukee Public Library, Golda Meir Library at University of Wisconsin-Milwaukee, and Milwaukee County Historical Society helped me research a number of buildings. Kristin Visser, my publisher, deserves special recognition and thanks for her foresight, patience, and trust. Without her, my manuscript would be just that.

Lastly, I must give a big thanks to Sandy, Becky, and Rachel for their love, help, and understanding during the years of this project.

About This Book

Milwaukee's downtown is the most architecturally important two square miles in the state of Wisconsin; its diversity and skyline are unequaled. The city is home to over 600,000 people. Its 96 square miles encompass more than 150,000 buildings, only 150 of which are discussed here. Buildings were selected for this book based on architectural merit, historic value, and overall importance to the community. Some are featured because of their visibility; they are those buildings that one often sees but knows little about. Other recognized landmarks simply could not be excluded. Perhaps a structure was included because its architect introduced a new style, explored new materials, or challenged conventional techniques. The selection was indifferent to the celebrity status of individual architects or architectural firms. These 150 buildings reveal much about the changing nature of Milwaukee as it grew from a village into a great city.

Milwaukee Architecture explores five geographic areas. Each chapter begins with a map keyed to a list of buildings that are significant in that part of the city. Discussions of each building follows. Each includes current name of the building, its address, the architect or firm that designed it, the location of the architect or firm, the year it was completed and major renovation data when applicable. The text describes the building or group and discusses architectural style, size, materials, and its significance. Buildings are listed in an order that allows for a self-guided walking or driving tour in each area.

This book is not intended to be all-inclusive, but, rather, can serve as a point of departure, as an impetus for further exploration into the architecture of the Cream City. Readers should be inspired to search out other buildings that they consider significant.

Included in *Milwaukee Architecture* are 59 buildings that were completed in the nineteenth century. Of these, 45 were designed by Milwaukee architects or architect/builders. Four were drawn by nonlocal talent, and ten were designed by persons unknown. For some of

Milwaukee's earliest buildings, it is impossible to acknowledge a specific architect or firm. In many cases no "architects" were involved, at least not by modern definition. Records of those early years are elusive, and any irrefutable proof is difficult to come by.

By contrast, the post-World War II era offers more accessible and accurate architectural information. Of the fifty buildings featured in the text that were built after 1945, twenty-five were designed by architects outside of Milwaukee. By then, access to national firms was easier, competition from distant architects was greater, and corporate loyalty to a single local firm vanished. Consequently, Milwaukee's architecture became less regional and more sophisticated. The principal architects of seven of the city's ten tallest buildings were not from Wisconsin. The city's skyline thus owes much of its appearance to out-of-state architects.

Joseph Korom
Milwaukee, December 1994

Guided Tours

Reference to a structure does not constitute an invitation to visit. Permission (especially in the case of residential properties) should be obtained beforehand from owner or occupant.

Public and government buildings are open during usual business hours, and their rules of entry should be observed.

The following buildings offer public tours. Please call for the most current information.

Annunciation Greek Orthodox Church, (414) 461-9400

Haggerty Museum of Art, (414) 288-1669

Miller Brewery, (414) 931-2337

Milwaukee Art Museum, (414) 224-3225

Milwaukee County Historical Society, (414) 273-8288

Mitchell Park Conservatory (the Domes), (414) 649-9800

Pabst Brewery, (414) 223-3709

Captain Frederick Pabst Mansion, (414) 931-0808

Pabst Theater, (414) 286-3665

St. Josaphat Basilica, (414) 645-5623

Pabst Building, once Milwaukee's tallest building.
Solon Spencer Beman, 1892. Demolished 1981.

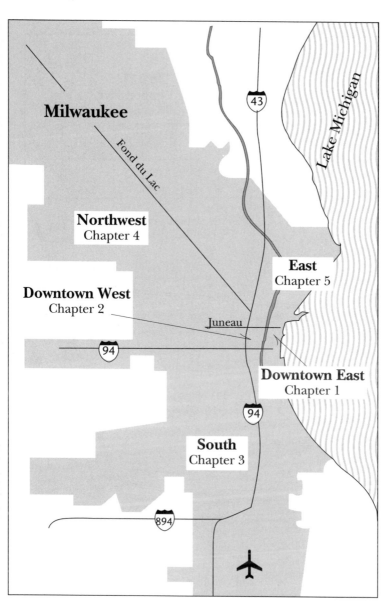

Guide to the Maps

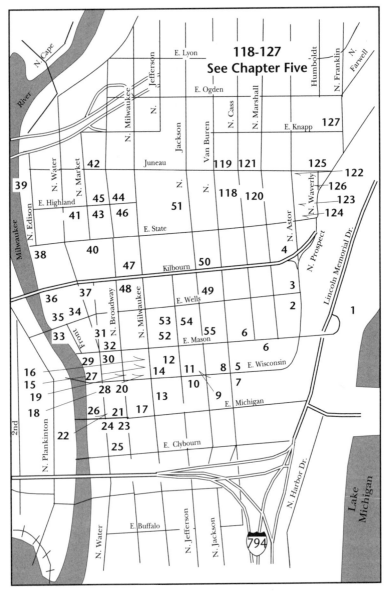

Downtown East

Chapter One
Downtown East

Situated between Lake Michigan and the Milwaukee River is the eastern half of downtown Milwaukee. What has become a collection of tightly knit neighborhoods began as a pioneer settlement founded by Solomon Juneau in 1835. Juneau, and later others, constructed cabins, stores, and a fur trading post at what is presently the heart of downtown Milwaukee. The downtown we have inherited, and which we view today, is the result of some 160 years of development.

Originally called Juneautown, the area was already eleven years old when Milwaukee was incorporated as a city in 1846. The new city was filled with European immigrants searching for opportunities that a place like Milwaukee provided. By 1850, there were substantial brick homes, churches, hotels, banks, schools, tanneries, grain warehouses, saloons, and, of course, breweries.

Streets were laid out on a grid between the river and the lake. There were boat docks on the river, and piers extended into the lake. Milwaukee's first City Hall was constructed in 1852 on the site of the present building. The Milwaukee Court House of 1872 was also located on downtown's east side. Banks, law offices, and insurance companies crowded the blocks around these government buildings. As a result, early versions of the skyscraper arose.

Today downtown east is home to nine of the ten tallest buildings in the state. The area is studded with significant structures, an impressive mix of architectural styles, and buildings of national importance.

Downtown east is Wisconsin's principal business hub, encompassing the headquarters of some of the state's largest insurance, banking, and corporate concerns. In addition, it is a retail mecca and home to fine hotels and restaurants, elegant residences, major cultural and educational institutions, and government offices.

Downtown East Buildings

1   War Memorial Center/Milwaukee Art Museum
2   Cudahy Tower
3   University Club
4   Regency House Condominiums
5   Northwestern Mutual Life Building
6   Northwestern Mutual Life Complex
7   Firstar Center
8   Wisconsin Gas Building
9   American National Bank Building
10   Milwaukee Federal Building
11   Milwaukee Club
12   Pfister Hotel
13   411 East Wisconsin Center
14   Curry-Pierce Block, Small Block
15   Bowman Block, Bowman's Row
16   James Conroy Building
17   McGeoch Building
18   Wells Building
19   Wisconsin Bell Telephone Building
20   Railway Exchange Building
21   611 Building
22   Insurance Exchange Building
23   Grain Exchange Building
24   Mitchell Building
25   Button Block
26   Bank One Plaza
27   100 East Building
28   Iron Block
29   First National Bank Building
30   Water Street Parking Tower
31   Marshall & Ilsley Bank Building
32   222 East Mason Street Building
33   Fine Arts Building
34   Pabst Theater
35   Milwaukee Repertory Powerhouse Theater
36   Milwaukee Center
37   Milwaukee City Hall
38   Performing Arts Center
39   River Houses Condominiums

Cherub, Milwaukee City Hall, 200 East Wells Street,
H. C. Koch & Co., 1895.

1. War Memorial Center
750 North Lincoln Memorial Drive
Eero Saarinen, Ann Arbor, Michigan
Maynard Meyer, Milwaukee   1957

Milwaukee Art Museum
Kahler, Slater and Fitzhugh Scott, Milwaukee   1975

What appears to be one building is actually two—
the War Memorial Center above and Art Museum below
are housed in stacked concrete boxes. Finnish-born architect Eero Saarinen (1910-1961), designer of the Gateway
Arch (1965) in St. Louis, created this elevated structure of
beige reinforced concrete resting on pylons and cantilevered in four directions. Individually, the War Memorial and the Art Museum are clear and restrained architectural expressions. Together they have a synergistic effect—
the dynamic shape of the War Memorial contrasts with the
static properties of the "museum pedestal" below.

The War Memorial Center, housing offices and
meeting rooms, surrounds a courtyard containing an eter-
nal flame, reflecting pool, and the inscribed names of Milwaukee's war dead. A large mosaic occupies the west face
of the building. Executed by the Milwaukee artist Edmund
Lewandowski, the abstract mosaic contains Roman numer-
als representing the years America was involved in World
War II and the Korean War. This brightly colored artwork
hints at the art collection in the adjoining museum.

4

Until the opening of the Milwaukee Art Museum, the city's entire public art collection was housed in the lower floors of the War Memorial Center. Before 1957, when the consolidation of the Layton Gallery and the Milwaukee Art Institute occurred, the artworks were kept in various buildings throughout the city. By the early 1970s, a fund drive provided the money necessary for expansion of the War Memorial Center to include a separate, but attached, structure for the art collection. Many local individuals and businesses were responsible for the creation of the Milwaukee Art Museum, but none deserves more credit than Mrs. Harry Lynde Bradley. As early as 1968, she decided to give her extensive art collection to the public, provided it could be properly housed. In addition, she and the Allen-Bradley Foundation contributed the funds for the new building. In September 1975, the Milwaukee Art Museum opened to the public.

Milwaukee architect David Kahler was called upon for the delicate task of adding onto a structure designed by a world-famous architect and located at what is described as Milwaukee's "front door." The result was nothing less than masterful.

The Milwaukee Art Museum measures 200 feet square and extends close to the lake's edge. Like the War Memorial Center, it is built of reinforced concrete, and its lake facade has deeply inset windows. The museum contains 94,000 square feet of exhibit space on three floors and houses a collection of more than 15,000 works. The lower level of the museum is 15 feet below the water level of Lake Michigan. The museum does not stand on pilings but rests upon a two-foot-thick reinforced concrete slab designed not only to support the building above but to

withstand the tremendous pressure of the upward-pushing water.

The Milwaukee Art Museum also houses a multimedia theater, a cafe, and storage, curatorial, and office areas. A sculpture court and rooftop promenade allow visitors to enjoy the geometric lines of the War Memorial Center above as well as an unobstructed view of the lake.

2. Cudahy Tower
925 East Wells Street
Ferry & Clas, Milwaukee   1909
Holabird & Root, Chicago   1929
James McClintock, Milwaukee   1987

The Cudahy Tower is actually two buildings. In 1909, meat-packer and philanthropist Patrick Cudahy built Milwaukee's tallest (seven stories) and most luxurious apartment building. It stands on the southern part of this site.

By 1929, Cudahy's sons erected the tallest apartment building at the time in Milwaukee, on land adjacent to, and north of, the original. It contains 150 apartments.

Forming a T in plan, the structure rises eleven floors. At the crossing there emerges a five-story tower with a pyramidal cap. The buildings are a restrained interpretation of the Italian Renaissance style. They are sheathed in white marble and glazed brick, and their facades are adorned with decorative terra cotta.

In 1987, the 84 apartments in the 1909 building were converted into 39 award-winning condominium units. New penthouses, with outdoor terraces, were created. All exterior surfaces were restored and interiors luxuriously appointed with modern conveniences.

3. University Club
924 East Wells Street
John Russell Pope, New York City   1926

Occupying a prestigious lakeside location, this private club building offers a Georgian Revival facade, an uncommon style for downtown Milwaukee. The University Club is faced with red brick and trimmed in Bedford lime-

stone. Three-story pilasters and a stone balustrade encircling the fifth floor reinforce the Georgian look. A copper-faced cocktail lounge, designed by Milwaukee architect Elliott B. Mason in 1953, tops the building.

The Georgian Revival style was popular in America during the 1920s, especially among upper income families. Their homes echoed the formal elegance of country estates such as those of Jeffersonian Virginia, and to some, symbolized affluence and carefree, Gatsby-like social affairs. Georgian Revival was the perfect image for a private club frequented by industrialists, executives, bankers, and those of substantial means.

Architect John Russell Pope (1874-1937) was known for his many distinguished classical buildings, such as the National Archives (1933-1935), the National Gallery of Art (1937-1941), and the Jefferson Memorial (1937-1943).

4. Regency House Condominiums
929 North Astor Street
Joel Hillman, Chicago   1969

The 27-story Regency House is downtown Milwaukee's tallest residential building. It features 200 luxury condominiums, an outdoor pool, a penthouse, and underground parking. All corner units have circular balconies that afford spectacular views of the city and Lake Michigan. Facades are composed of brown-orange brick and bronze-tinted windows. Its contemporary style recalls the apartment towers of Chicago's lakefront.

5. Northwestern Mutual Life Building
720 East Wisconsin Avenue
Marshall & Fox, Chicago   1914

This architectural masterpiece is the headquarters and home office of one of America's largest insurance companies, Northwestern Mutual Life, as well as one of Milwaukee's great landmarks.

The Mutual Life Insurance Company of Wisconsin was founded in Janesville in 1857, moved to Milwaukee in 1859, and changed its name to Northwestern Mutual Life Insurance Company by 1865. Northwestern Mutual occupied a series of offices in downtown Milwaukee beginning with the Iron Block (1862-1870), then the Broadway Building (1870-1886, now demolished), and finally the structure now known simply as the 611 Building (1886-1914). In 1914, the company moved one last time.

Through much of the nineteenth century, the area that is now the 700 block of East Wisconsin Avenue was a spring-fed lake. Lake Emily, as it was called, was filled in, and houses quickly sprang up at this desirable location. After purchasing the site and clearing the land, Northwestern Mutual began to erect its headquarters building.

In 1912, construction commenced on what was to become the largest office building on Milwaukee's east side to date. Over 6,000 wood piles had to be driven into the earth to provide a solid foundation atop the former lake. Thousands of tons of steel and granite were delivered to the site, and by October 1914, the great building was completed.

This eight-story neoclassical structure is dressed in white granite. The main facade is a wall of copper sheeting

and glass, the copper pressed into classical-motif low relief. In front, ten 74-foot Corinthian columns march boldly across the building's main elevation.

A central entrance and steps, flanked by classical light standards, lead to a breathtaking temple-like lobby. This interior space, a "corporate temple a la Rome," is a masterpiece of design. A coffered marble ceiling, pairs of stairways framed by Ionic columns, pedimented doorways, and Doric-inspired pilasters dignify the room. Marble from Spain, Italy, Alabama, and Tennessee is generously used throughout the building.

The architectural firm Marshall & Fox was founded in 1905 by Benjamin H. Marshall (1874-1945) and Charles E. Fox (1870-1926). Together Marshall and Fox designed many notable buildings, including such leading Chicago hotels as the Blackstone (1910), the Morrison (1915), the Drake (1919), and the Edgewater Beach (1921).

6. Northwestern Mutual Life Complex
Northwestern Mutual Life Place
815 East Mason Street
Poor, Swanke, Hayden & Connell, New York City
Sasaki Associates, Watertown, Massachusetts   1979

Northwestern Mutual Life Data Center
818 East Mason Street
Beckley, Meyers, Flad & Associates, Milwaukee   1990

Immediately northeast of the neoclassical headquarters building is Northwestern Mutual Life Place, a 16-
story, auburn-hued tower. The building's exterior is faced
with carnelian (reddish) granite and bronze-tinted glass. A
skywalk connects the tower to a dramatic six-story atrium
located on the north side of the original Marshall & Fox
building.

The 18-story, half-million-square-foot Northwestern
Mutual Life Data Center is the northernmost building and
the latest addition to the NML complex. Gray granite and
tinted glass wrap this tower, which contains data process-
ing services and other company offices. Housing the building's mechanical systems is a pyramidal top, which, along
with the tower's summit, is dramatically lighted at night.
Some 2,500 people work in the three buildings.

The architecture of these three buildings illustrates

America's changing values in aesthetics over the last 70 years. When the original neoclassical structure was built, the look of ancient Rome was the favored architectural style of government, banks, and insurance companies. By the 1970s the symbolic imagery of ancient Rome was long out of architectural favor. When it came time to build again, Northwestern Mutual Life chose modern icons to say something about Milwaukee, its company and employees, and the prevailing culture. This time, it chose streamlined skyscrapers.

7. Firstar Center
777 East Wisconsin Avenue
Skidmore, Owings and Merrill, Chicago
Fitzhugh Scott Architects, Milwaukee   1973

Firstar Center is Wisconsin's biggest and tallest office building, headquarters for Wisconsin's largest banking company, and home to hundreds of business tenants. Standing 42 floors (601 feet), it contains 1.4 million square feet of floor space, the equivalent of seven city blocks. Excavation for the Firstar Center began in April 1971, and the building was dedicated on October 6, 1973.

The Firstar Center is an excellent example of the International style. The crisp, geometric tower rises from a two-level, glass-enclosed podium, which contains a main banking area and The Galleria, a landscaped public area of restaurants and shops. Some seven million pounds of Italian travertine stone were used throughout the Center, more than in any other building in the state. This stone was quarried in the area surrounding Tivoli, Italy, 30 miles east of Rome and is the same type of stone used on St. Peter's Basilica and the Colosseum in Rome. Two abstract paintings by world-renowned artist Helen Frankenthaler (born New York City, 1928) adorn the main banking area inside the Wisconsin Avenue entrance. These 80-by-22-foot acrylic-on-canvas paintings contribute color to an otherwise monochromatic space.

The exterior skin of Firstar Center consists of 66 percent glass and 34 percent white silicone-polyester-coated aluminum. Its 5,000 double-glazed windows range in

thickness from 3/4-inch on the lower floors, to 1-1/8-inch at the top; thicker glass is required at the top where the winds are stronger. The exterior diagonal trusses mark the mechanical equipment levels on floors 15-16 and 41-42. Requirements for the curtain wall skin of the structure specified that it be able to withstand a "100-year wind," the strongest wind that might occur in a 100-year period in Milwaukee. That was found to be 90 miles per hour at grade level. Extensive tests of the curtain wall showed that it could withstand winds of more than 180 miles per hour.

To keep the tower's windows clean, automatic window-washing machines glide up and down through channels in the exterior walls. Traveling at 45 feet per minute, the machine takes about 34 minutes to complete a round trip between the Center's fourth and fortieth floors. The machine holds 20 gallons of water, plus cleaning agents, washing brushes, and a vacuum. It takes about 50 hours to wash all the windows.

8. Wisconsin Gas Building
626 East Wisconsin Avenue
Eschweiler & Eschweiler, Milwaukee   1930

The 20-story Wisconsin Gas Building is Milwaukee's finest Art Deco skyscraper and one of the best examples of this style anywhere. This tower is a masterpiece of form, of sensitive scale, and of urbanity. Its distinctive ziggurat shape, recalling early Babylonian or Mayan designs, was influenced by the stepped-back-style towers of 1920s Manhattan.

This office building, with its cascading masses, is embellished by jazzy brick patterns, Deco terra-cotta friezes, and zigzags etched into its granite trim. Metal spandrels in low relief depict sunbursts, foliate patterns, the building's profile, and the letters MGL, which recall the company's original name, Milwaukee Gas Light. It is faced in an orange brick that progressively becomes lighter in color as the building rises, which gives the effect of greater height and seems to catch the sunlight on an overcast day.

Atop the building is a 21-foot-tall plastic "weather flame." This famous flame contains hundreds of feet of neon- and argon-filled tubes and, when lit, forecasts the weather. Red signals warmer, gold means colder, and blue predicts no temperature change. A flashing flame forecasts precipitation. When this beautiful structure is lighted at night, it is a romantic landmark, visible for miles.

9. American National Bank Building
526 East Wisconsin Avenue
Ferry & Clas, Milwaukee   1906

The American National Bank Building is one of Milwaukee's finest remaining examples of Beaux Arts architecture. Built as the home office and headquarters of the Northwestern National Insurance Company, today it is the headquarters of another Milwaukee financial services company, the American National Bank.

Humble in size but robust in style, the limestone facades exhibit such design devices as two-story fluted Ionic columns, carved-stone grotesques, wrought bronze grillwork, and a classical entablature. Above, a copper-trimmed third floor is tucked into an orange terra-cotta-tiled mansard roof. The ornately trimmed windows are styled in true Beaux Arts fashion.

10. Milwaukee Federal Building
517 East Wisconsin Avenue
Willoughby J. Edbrooke, Washington D.C.
Bernard Kolpacki, Milwaukee   1899

This landmark building is one of the finest examples of Richardsonian Romanesque architecture in America. It reinterprets the great stone architecture of medieval Europe, particularly that of southern France and Spain. The supervising architect of the United States Treasury Department, Willoughby J. Edbrooke (1843-1896), responded with this design when Milwaukee petitioned for a new federal office building and courthouse.

The Milwaukee Federal Building, which required seven years for construction, occupies an entire city block. It is faced with alternating courses of smoothly cut and rusticated Maine-quarried granite. Its composition successfully incorporates pavilions, arches, towers, gables, and copper-topped turrets. Facades are embellished with foliate patterns, 78 human faces, 14 monster gargoyles, and 12 winged dragons, four of which breathe fire! A bold foursquare tower, resembling a medieval watchtower, rises 190 feet above the mass of the building.

The main entrance leads to a domed, mosaic-covered vestibule with a terrazzo floor. Inside, an immense light court, topped by an iron and glass skylight, is ringed by open corridors, government offices, and richly appointed courtrooms.

In 1931, a southern addition to the building was completed. Its granite facades and arches complement the design of the original Romanesque-inspired building.

Architect Edbrooke was born in England, immigrated to America as a youth, and settled in Chicago, where he began his architectural practice in 1867. In 1892, he was appointed by President Harrison to the post of supervising architect of the U. S. Treasury Department, a national position from which he was to help design and oversee all new federal office buildings. One of those, the celebrated post office in Washington, D.C., was designed in the same style as the Milwaukee Federal Building and completed the same year, 1899.

11. Milwaukee Club
706 North Jefferson Street
Edward Townsend Mix, Milwaukee   1883

This building, erected as a private business/social club, is a superb example of Queen Anne architecture. Its asymmetrical facades have bay windows, steep and multi-

ple roofs that frequently intersect, and tall multiple chimneys. A variety of surface textures include sandstone, red brick, terra cotta, and slate. Ornamental cast-iron railings depict floral, sunburst, and pea pod designs. On the southwest corner rises a five-sided tower capped by a bell-shaped cupola. This landmark remains the home of the club that erected it.

12. Pfister Hotel

424 East Wisconsin Avenue
Henry C. Koch and Herman J. Esser, Milwaukee   1893
Rasche, Schroeder, Spransy & Associates, Milwaukee 1965

Milwaukee's oldest hotel, this eight-story landmark has become one of the premier hotels in the Midwest and is one of the few designed in the Richardson Romanesque style. The 150-room hotel was planned by businessman Guido Pfister (1818-1889) and completed by his son Charles (1859-1927).

The Pfister's facades of rusticated limestone and Cream City brick are trimmed with terra-cotta decoration. Oriel windows, balustraded balconies, and stained glass also add to the composition. The interior features a stunning three-story barrel-vaulted Victorian lobby. This space was restored to its nineteenth century elegance in 1993 and is not to be missed!

Architect Herman J. Esser was credited with many of the modern conveniences, including electric elevators, incorporated into this building. Esser (1865-1957) was born in Madison, Wisconsin, and studied architecture at Cornell University. He interned in New York City and opened an office in Milwaukee in 1890. Henry C. Koch was a more seasoned designer who had drawn the plans for dozens of homes and businesses by the time he worked on the Pfister.

A 1965 expansion of the hotel added an eight-story garage beneath a 157-room, 13-story tower.

13. 411 East Wisconsin Center

411 East Wisconsin Avenue

Harry Weese & Associates, Chicago   1985

This 30-story, six-sided rhomboid adds a skewed dimension to Milwaukee's skyline. The 600,000-square-foot office building rises 374 feet; its perimeter measures 675 feet. Structurally, the 411 Center is a beige pillar with a poured-in-place concrete core and skeleton. The facades consist of 1,200 precast concrete panels, each of which weighs eight tons. The tower's thousands of bronze-tinted windows have been deeply inset to enhance the effect of shadow, a crucial design element on what might ordinarily be considered a deadening concrete mass. Each window's concrete frame has a chamfered edge for added shadow emphasis. The 411 Center's design, which can be described as contemporary minimalist, abolishes symbols and decoration; it produces the container without the cultural baggage.

A two-story banking hall fronting on Wisconsin

Avenue is connected to the tower via a five-tiered, glass-enclosed atrium.

Integral to the design of this skyscraper is a nine-level, 1,000-car parking pavilion, which is used by many of the 3,000 who work or visit the building each day.

14. Curry-Pierce Block
404 East Wisconsin Avenue
architect unknown   1866
David Kaul, Oconomowoc, Wisconsin   1993

Small Block
706-708 North Milwaukee Street
Edward Townsend Mix, Milwaukee   1866

The Curry-Pierce Block was constructed in 1866 as two separate, three-story, Italianate business buildings. James Curry built the eastern portion of this now-joined building. Curry was a confectioner who made and sold pastries, candy, and other delicacies. His neighbor Amos J. W. Pierce (1832-1917), a grocer who was also a respected commodity trader, built the western half of this commercial development.

In 1879, the fourth and fifth floors were added, and the two buildings were joined. The Curry-Pierce Block's mansard roof was, of course, part of the 1879 addition,

and it reflects that period's preference for the French Second Empire style.

Milwaukee's TMB Development renovated the Curry-Pierce Block in 1993. The interior was completely modernized for banking and office space, and the exterior brick was cleaned and painted to resemble Cream City brick.

Immediately north of and abutting Curry-Pierce is the Italianate Small Block, built by attorney Simeon Small (1821-1875) in 1866. The facade focuses on a central pavilion topped by a pediment. Window arrangements are a variation on the Palladian theme; the center window of each grouping is topped by an arch-and-scallop motif, which recalls the Italian Baroque. Brick quoins bracket the three-story Cream City brick building, which is topped by a delicate cornice and a stone plaque bearing the year 1866. Shortly after completion, celebrated architect Edward Townsend Mix moved his office here.

15. Bowman Block
715-717 North Milwaukee Street
Edward Townsend Mix, Milwaukee 1860

Bowman's Row
719-723 North Milwaukee Street
Edward Townsend Mix, Milwaukee 1874

The Bowman Block, a marvelous example of Italianate commercial architecture, was built by George Bowman (1809-1874) to house his successful dry goods business. This is one of the few antebellum business buildings surviving in downtown Milwaukee. Its Cream City brick walls are remarkably well preserved and still display hood moldings above the windows, a bracketed cornice at roof level, and a decorated pediment.

In 1874, George Bowman again called upon architect Edward Townsend Mix to design the adjoining Bowman's Row. This three-story office/retail structure is a two-building development that shares a common supporting wall. The Row was also constructed of Cream City brick in Italianate style, and has pronounced window hood moldings and bracketed cornices.

16. James Conroy Building

725-729 North Milwaukee Street
architect unknown   1881

The Conroy Building epitomizes the robust aspects of Queen Anne commercial architecture. Originally headquarters for a catering company, the three-story building is topped by an attic. The facade is balanced by two large window bays. At the second-floor level is a carved plaque with the year 1881, intermingled with a pot of blooming flowers and lush leaves. Carved lion heads, decorative brickwork and terra cotta, and a variety of textures, materials, and window styles add to the picturesque aspects of this landmark. The Conroy Building was listed in an 1886 French guide as one of America's 120 most significant buildings. Sadly, much of the original first floor exterior has been erased by remodelings.

17. McGeoch Building
322 East Michigan Street
Eugene Liebert, Milwaukee   1895

This six-story building is located in what was known at the turn of the century as Milwaukee's printing and newspaper row. Other buildings that housed printing companies and newspapers, such as *The Milwaukee Journal* and the *Evening Wisconsin*, have been demolished. This is the lone survivor in an area now peppered by high-rises and parking decks.

The McGeoch (pronounced "mc-gee-oh") Building is faced with tan brick, trimmed with terra cotta, and wrapped with a sheet metal cornice. The fifth-floor windows are arched, and pilasters are capped with Ionic capitals in a style best termed Renaissance Commercial.

Interestingly, both Michigan Street entrances have cast-iron stairways, which are rare in the Midwest. The iron steps have blue glass discs pressed into the risers and dis-

play the foundry's name in raised letters: J. G. Wagner Iron Works, Mil. Wis.

Peter McGeoch, a dabbler in stocks and a speculator in commodities futures, built this handsome office building for investment income. His investments were often careless, his business dealings erratic, and his personal life stormy. In 1895, shortly after seeing the McGeoch Building completed, he committed suicide.

Architect Liebert (1866-1945) was born and educated in Germany. He arrived in Milwaukee in 1883 and in 1890 established an architectural partnership with fellow German Herman Schnetzky that lasted until 1897.

18. Wells Building
324 East Wisconsin Avenue
H. C. Koch and Company, Milwaukee   1901

The 15-story Wells Building was one of Milwaukee's first skyscrapers and one of the first to have electric elevators. Upon completion, it was reportedly the largest terra-

cotta-covered building in the world.

The first two floors are faced with copper and large panes of glass, while the upper floors are of white glazed terra cotta and cream-colored brick. Its Renaissance-inspired design features an impressive two-story arched entrance, mosaics, and stringcourses supporting carved wolf heads, eagles, and owls. Unfortunately, the top four floors were stripped of their detailing, and the building's rooftop cornice was removed due to structural problems.

The building was named for Daniel Wells, Jr., who was born in Maine in 1802, and moved to the pioneer village of Milwaukee in 1836. He worked as a surveyor, probate judge, and county supervisor, and served a term in the U.S. Congress. His business dealings involved real estate, insurance, banking, railroads and shipping. When he died in 1902, a year after completion of the building, Wells was thought to be the wealthiest man in Wisconsin.

19. Wisconsin Bell Telephone Building
722 North Broadway
Eschweiler & Eschweiler, Milwaukee   1930

This site was once occupied by the city's first hotel, the Milwaukee House, built by pioneer Solomon Juneau and an associate in 1835. Across from the hotel, on the west side of Broadway, a four-story commercial building was erected in 1869 and later housed the Milwaukee Telephone Exchange Company, founded in 1879. When the telephone's popularity made larger quarters necessary, the Milwaukee House was demolished to make way for a five-story structure, completed in 1891. Resembling a sixteenth-century European guild hall, it was a substantial structure of steel, brick, and terra cotta with a sloping tile roof. In 1916, it was leveled, along with the building next door, to make way for a new headquarters building.

The skyscraper that stands today is the product of two additions to an eight-story structure that was completed in 1917. With the addition of five floors in 1924 and three more in 1930, the building appeared as it does today, a 16-story office block faced with orange brick, trimmed with tan terra cotta, and capped by three penthouse floors and a massive hipped copper roof. It is an important example of 1920s architecture, which drew on historical European forms in experiments in design of that wholly American invention, the skyscraper.

The building is an interpretation of French Chateauesque style. Rising like a Norman castle, the central tower, complete with bay windows, is romantic and inspiring. Moorish-style turrets cap each corner. Argyle-patterned brickwork above the nineteenth floor is the only break in the severe and symmetrical main facade.

On the roof is a large lantern that once housed four powerful beacons. Each of the four lamps had 200,000 candlepower and was visible nightly for a distance of twenty miles. The beacons no longer shine; the lantern is illuminated from within, and the tower is floodlighted at night.

Two office wings jut eastward, forming a U-shaped design that allows access to sunlight and fresh air for all offices. An unusual feature is a bridge that connects the two wings at the thirteenth-floor level.

20. Railway Exchange Building
233 East Wisconsin Avenue
Jenney & Mundie, Chicago
Herman Buemming, Milwaukee   1901

This 12-story skyscraper was built by real estate businessman Henry Herman to house law, insurance, and railroad concerns. It is the only skyscraper outside Chicago that was designed by the celebrated Jenney & Mundie firm.

The Railway Exchange, a fine example of the Renaissance Revival style, is vertically divided into clearly defined base, middle, and top. Its facades are covered with Italian Renaissance detailing, such as a large arched entrance of stone that is trimmed in egg-and-dart and garland drapings. Terra-cotta cartouches, dentils, and two-story classical columns are also employed. Sadly, its decorative cornice was removed. It is interesting that Jenney & Mundie looked to the Renaissance for Milwaukee's Railway Exchange after having designed other structures that

were considered more modern looking. The Railway Exchange used "modern" technology on the inside, while its exterior reflects a more conservative approach.

William Le Baron Jenney is credited with drawing the plans for the world's first skyscraper, Chicago's 10-story Home Insurance Building (1884), which used an iron and steel skeleton, brick and glass curtain wall, and electric lights and elevators. Fifteen years later, Milwaukee's Railway Exchange was designed using the same modern technology as its famous forerunner.

21. 611 Building
611 North Broadway
Solon Spencer Beman, Chicago   1886

Originally built as the headquarters for the Northwestern Mutual Life Insurance Company, this robust six-story office block is a superb example of Richardsonian Romanesque architecture. The exterior is a skillful blend of glass and large blocks of roughly hewn gray granite. Polished marble columns framing the main entrance support heavily carved capitals and a beautiful arch. A carved spandrel above the entrance, reading *Organized A.D. 1852, Erected A.D. 1886*, refers to the founding of Northwestern Mutual Life and to the completion of this building. Street facades, girded by 72 stone arches, recall the architecture

of eighth-century European monasteries and fortresses.

The 611 Building has one of the most magnificent interiors in Wisconsin, featuring colorful marble walls, decorative iron newel posts (capped by spiked, polished copper finials), and two-story iron columns. Dazzling ceramic tile patterns in the floor form a colorful nineteenth-century tapestry. A light court, surrounded by office windows and elevators, rises from the second floor to a great glass and iron canopy, a web of trusses, and more than 2,000 translucent glass squares that allow sunlight into this grand space.

22. Insurance Exchange Building
210 East Michigan Street
Mygatt & Schmidtner, Milwaukee   1856
Albert Nash, Milwaukee   1858

This four-story antebellum structure was originally two separate buildings. The western half was completed in 1856 as the State Bank of Wisconsin; the eastern half was built in 1858 as the Bank of Milwaukee. Today, they are considered one structure and recognized as Milwaukee's oldest bank building.

The Insurance Exchange Building, designed in Venetian Renaissance style, is a superb example of a mid-

nineteenth-century business block. The building is faced with skillfully carved limestone blocks, but unfortunately the western portion has been stripped of much original detail. The eastern half abounds with carvings of rose bouquets, seashells, and Byzantine-inspired busts. The arched and pedimented main entrance is flanked by rope-twist stone columns with Renaissance capitals, and is surmounted by a stone tablet reading simply Bank. A first-floor window pediment is supported by two tall iron colonettes whose iron capitals are in the shape of giant sunflowers.

The architects of the western portion of this building, George W. Mygatt (1820-1883) and Leon Alfons Schmidtner (1825-1875), founded one of Milwaukee's earliest architectural firms. Ohioan Albert C. Nash (1826-1890), designer of the eastern half of the Insurance Exchange, was one of Cincinnati's first architects.

Mygatt designed many of the city's homes, business blocks, and hotels during the 1840s and 1850s. He also trained many draftsmen, one of whom was Henry C. Koch, who later became Mygatt's partner.

23. Grain Exchange Building
225 East Michigan Street
Edward Townsend Mix, Milwaukee   1879

The Grain Exchange is a Victorian landmark built to house what was once the world's largest grain exchange and the offices of firms that bought and sold commodities. Businessman Alexander Mitchell built both the Grain Exchange and the neighboring Mitchell Building.

Merchants and brokers came here to speculate in wheat, corn, soybeans, and other products. The great trading room rises three floors and occupies an area 60 by 115 feet. This Italian Renaissance-style space is rich with frescoes, stained glass, columns, arches, stenciling, and carvings. The architecture and strong colors of the interior fuse into a burst of unmatched Victorian dazzle.

In the years just after the Civil War, Milwaukee exported more wheat than any other port in the world, and at this busy commodity exchange the octagonal trading pit was invented.

Various trading pits (lowered floors encircled by a series of rising steps where traders gathered) were located

on the floor of the great trading room. Large wooden tables, piled high with samples of the grains for inspection by brokers, stood nearby.

The Grain Exchange's six-story facade is faced with limestone and granite decorated with gargoyles, allegorical figures, and other Renaissance-inspired ornaments. Wisconsin's state seal and motto are visible, as are a carved bull and bear, symbolic stock market indicators. Mercury, the Roman god of trade, commerce, and travel, is prominently poised at the main entrance; the nineteenth century is represented by reliefs of a steamship and locomotive. The carved words Chamber of Commerce refer to a one-time tenant of the building.

Above the office block rises a square 175-foot tower containing a one-ton bell and capped by a copper-clad cupola. Gargoyles guard each corner of this campanile, whose bell no doubt rang to signal the arrival of such dignitaries as Grand Duke Alexis of Russia and Presidents William Taft and Theodore Roosevelt.

24. Mitchell Building
207 East Michigan Street
Edward Townsend Mix, Milwaukee 1876

The Mitchell Building is one of the country's finest examples of French Second Empire architecture, a style based upon Parisian buildings designed during the reign of Louis Napoleon.

Alexander Mitchell's (1817-1887) bank and railroad and lumber concerns were originally housed in this building. (It was Alexander Mitchell's grandson, Billy, who became a famous aviator, and after whom Milwaukee's Mitchell International Airport was named.)

A central pavilion boldly rising six floors to the elaborate mansard roof divides the symmetrical granite and limestone facade. Two gilded griffins guard the main entrance. Crisp carvings of allegorical figures, winged horses, seashells, lion heads, cherubs, garlands, and caryatids (female figures) all contribute to an energetic facade.

When completed the Mitchell Building, at 130 feet, was the second tallest building in Milwaukee; only the 174-foot Milwaukee Court House (1872), which once stood on Cathedral Square, was taller. The top floor of the Mitchell Building once housed the United States Signal Service, predecessor of the U.S. Weather Bureau.

The Mitchell Building stands on the site of Milwaukee pioneer Solomon Juneau's first house, built in 1835.

25. Button Block

500 North Water Street
Crane & Barkhausen, Milwaukee   1892

Charles Pearson Button, the owner of a Milwaukee knitting company, commissioned this handsome building, an important example of an office and light manufacturing building of the last century.

The seven-story, Romanesque-inspired building rests on a rusticated two-story sandstone base. The remainder of the building is a rich, red brick trimmed in a similarly colored terra cotta. The most interesting aspect of the Button Block is the delicately carved projecting turret, which is partially supported by a large granite column at the entrance. On the Water Street elevation, above the seventh-floor windows, a plaque reads A.D. Button Block 1892.

Architect Charles Crane (1850-1928) was born in New York, moved to Chicago in 1871, and then to Milwaukee in 1874, where he worked for Edward Townsend Mix.

Carl Barkhausen (1860-1934) was born in Thiensville, just north of Milwaukee, the son of German immigrants. At 16, he went to Germany to study architecture. Barkhausen also worked for E. T. Mix until 1888, when he and Crane formed their own firm.

With this strong German influence it is easy to see why the top of Crane & Barkhausen's Button Block recalls a German castle. This romantic and inspiring building is a valuable component of Milwaukee's skyline; few other turreted early high-rises remain.

26. Bank One Plaza
111 East Wisconsin Avenue
Harrison and Abramovitz, New York City   1961

The 22-story Bank One Plaza, Milwaukee's first glass-walled office skyscraper, is a powerful expression of the later phase of the International style. Its design, created on the drafting boards of one of the most successful and prolific architectural firms in New York City, is a prime example of 1950's "Manhattan chic."

Situated on the east bank of the Milwaukee River, this flat-topped, turquoise-green glass office tower colorfully complements the river, reflects the surrounding cityscape and sky, and serves as a counterpoint to nearby Victorian-era buildings. With alternating opaque and transparent glass panels separated by dark aluminum and

polished steel piers, the building is a giant rectilinear composition. Its exposed structural system is both functional and artistic.

When this building, originally known as the Marine Plaza, was completed by the Marine National Exchange Bank in 1961, it was the first new downtown high-rise in more than 30 years.

27. 100 East Building
100 East Wisconsin Avenue
Clark, Tribble, Harris, and Li, Charlotte, N.C.   1989

The 37-story 100 East Building is an excellent example of postmodern architecture. It was designed to recall one of Milwaukee's first skyscrapers, the 14-story Pabst Building (Solon Spencer Beman, 1892), which once stood

on this site. The postmodern style borrows freely from the past and reinterprets earlier architectural styles for contemporary buildings.

Levels three through nine provide parking for over 400 cars; floors 10 through 35 contain 400,000 square feet of office space. The top floors house the building's mechanical systems. A lower-level restaurant and riverwalk complement the tower's riverfront site.

Facades are faced with cream-colored Cordoba (Texas) limestone, chocolate-colored metal spandrel panels, and tinted glass. Arches, copper-clad Dutch gables with cresting, a cupola, and orbs figure prominently in the building's overall design. At the summit a 22-foot-diameter circular window marks the location of a law library tucked into the gabled roof. The 100 East Building is dramatically lighted at night and marks the heart of downtown Milwaukee.

Architects Clark, Tribble, Harris, and Li felt it important to emulate with this tower some of the characteristics of Milwaukee's historic Pabst Building. The honor bestowed upon the old Pabst by its "architectural resurrection" is somewhat dubious. Recalling historic architecture for contemporary purposes is fraught with difficulties of scale, symbolic meaning, culture, context, and technology. Though striking and considered romantic by some, Milwaukee's second tallest building perhaps needs the patina of age, a quality the demolished Pabst already possessed.

28. Iron Block
205 East Wisconsin Avenue
George H. Johnson, New York City   1861

The Iron Block is a landmark of special architectural significance. It belongs to a vanishing breed of American structures whose facades are entirely composed of cast iron. The Iron Block is an important link to an architectural genre of mass production, prefabrication, and superbly crafted Renaissance decoration.

Interior structure is of brick and timber with three-foot-thick bearing walls. The 120-foot-wide Wisconsin Avenue elevation is entirely composed of prefabricated cast-iron modules, bolted together to create the look of a Venetian Renaissance palazzo. Each pier, column, beam, and spandrel was cast in a foundry.

The Iron Block was financed and built by Baltimore-born businessman James Baynard Martin (1814-1878), who settled in Milwaukee in 1845. He established one of Milwaukee's first flour mills, bought real estate, organized the Farmers & Millers Bank (later named the First Wisconsin National Bank, and, most recently, Firstar), and traded in livestock and grain futures.

In 1860, Martin purchased this site and built a five-story business block for rental income and to house the Excelsior Lodge, a Masonic fraternity to which he belonged. Martin wanted an iron facade like those in Manhattan. He contacted Daniel Badger's Architectural Iron Works in New York City.

Daniel Badger (1806-1884) originally specialized in iron rolling shutters, but quickly began to fabricate entire cast-iron fronts for New York's loft, commercial, and office buildings. Badger was not an architect; his expertise was the foundry, metallurgy, and iron construction business.

English-born George H. Johnson (1830-1879), chief designer of Badger's newly created architectural depart-

ment, designed the Iron Block.

Milwaukee's Iron Block uses a simple cast-iron bay unit of Corinthian columns framing an arcade (occurring 66 times on the Iron Block), and has large display windows on the first floor. Construction of the Iron Block required that all iron components be bolted together and the entire front laid out on the floor of the foundry's fitting room in Manhattan. All parts were numbered and positioned in their respective locations as they were to appear on the building, and a protective paint applied to retard rust. The Iron Block's facades arrived in the summer of 1860, shipped by a schooner that tied up in the nearby Milwaukee River.

After the building's structural system of timber and brick was in place, the prefabricated iron modules were hauled by horse and wagon to the site for bolting to the underlying structure. This quick assembly process progressed upward from the first through the fifth floors. The result was a splendid iron box displaying fluted Corinthian columns, pediments, dentils, balustrades, and egg-and-dart-enriched stringcourses. The spandrels and piers were made to resemble blocks of stone, and iron lion heads glared downward, as if patiently carved by Renaissance craftsmen. The facades were painted white to resemble a marble-fronted palace of fifteenth-century Italy.

Cast iron offered several economic advantages. It was assembled more easily and quickly than conventional structures faced in stone. And regular painting was the only maintenance needed. These buildings were also supposed to be fireproof, but the iron facades tended to warp and collapse during intense fires.

Completed when Milwaukee was only 15 years old, the Excelsior Block, as it was originally known, was easily the largest office building in the city. The public referred to it as Martin's Iron Block and eventually it was renamed the Iron Block. Although the Iron Block appears to be a single structure, it is two. The south half was erected in 1891 as an annex and is faced with brick.

The Iron Block is Milwaukee's only cast-iron-fronted building and is one of only a handful outside of New York City. Manhattan has some 250 cast-iron-fronted buildings.

29. First National Bank Building
735 North Water Street
Daniel Burnham & Co. Chicago   1914

Squarely centered in the city's financial district, this 16-story office building has a classical appearance that helps maintain the area's formal character. Because of its size and location on a corner lot and the fact that it is not set back from the sidewalk, it contributes to the "canyon" look that prevails in downtown business sectors. The carved granite and brick walls envelop a structure that contains almost 400,000 square feet.

The building has three distinct parts. Sumptuously decorated lower levels surrender to plain, repetitive, mid-tower office floors. The whole pile is surmounted by a three-story crown that explodes with classical elements,

including huge carved stone urns, pilasters, copper-clad walls, and cornice.

The First National was erected as the home office of the First Wisconsin National Bank (renamed Firstar in 1992). It was headquartered here until 1973, when the Firstar Center was completed. This skyscraper is typical of those produced in the first two decades of this century. Classicism prevailed, especially for bank buildings, and every major city had at least one example.

30. Water Street Parking Tower
746 North Water Street
Martin Tullgren & Sons, Milwaukee   1929

This is one of the most unusual parking structures in America. It could easily pass for a large office building, since it is not girded by concrete ramps and resists the horizontal scheme used in virtually all multilevel parking decks.

The garage's Art Deco facades are decorated not with automobile designs but with terra-cotta sunflowers. Stressing the vertical, brick piers rise uninterrupted from the second floor to the roofline. Metal casement windows and first-floor businesses further reinforce the office tower imagery. The eight-story, 400-car Parking Tower rises from the sidewalk and maintains the traditional "business canyon" that is Water Street. This building is a perfect example of successfully inserting a new structure into an established context. It is a credit to Martin Tullgren's sensitivity.

31. Marshall & Ilsley Bank Building
770 North Water Street
Grassold-Johnson-Wagner & Isley, Milwaukee   1969

Providing a sharp visual contrast to neighboring Milwaukee City Hall and the Pabst Theater, the modern Marshall & Ilsley Bank is the headquarters for one of Wisconsin's largest banks, as well as the home office for other firms.

Box-like and devoid of any ornamentation, this 21-story structure can be seen as a massive, minimalist sculpture. The building's openings are narrow and recessed, making the tower appear as if it is windowless. Sunlight on the piers creates interesting shadow play on the facades.

The founders of the Marshall & Ilsley Bank were eastern businessmen Samuel Marshall and Charles Ilsley. They arrived independently in Milwaukee in 1847, the year in which Marshall founded S. Marshall & Company, a banking firm. Ilsley joined Marshall's bank in 1849, and the new firm was renamed the Marshall & Ilsley Bank.

32. 222 East Mason Street Building
222 East Mason Street
Architect unknown
East building: 1879   West building: 1884

Once separate buildings, these two Victorian structures were joined at the first floor, forming a "single building" in 1970. The east portion, once known as the Milwaukee News Building, was constructed in 1879 as headquar-

ters for a Democratic daily newspaper. In 1885, this building also became the home of the *Daily Journal*, later known as *The Milwaukee Journal*.

In 1884, the Milwaukee Abstract Association Building was erected to the west. It originally housed law offices as well as the *Wisconsin Legal News*, a daily report of official city and county activities.

These finely preserved office buildings are constructed with timber beams and columns and are faced with Cream City brick. The west half possesses a three-story bay with three distinctly different pediments capping sets of paired windows. Scrolls on the roofline proclaim the years 1884 (west) and 1879 (east).

33. Fine Arts Building
125 East Wells Street
Charles F. Ringer, Milwaukee   1891

The six-story Fine Arts Building is an excellent and well-preserved example of a nineteenth-century business

block. Faced with Cream City brick, this Italianate building is topped by a pronounced cornice and pediment.

In 1864, German-born Adolf Meinecke (1830-1905) built a factory to produce furniture, children's carriages, baskets, and toys on a site immediately to the south. In 1891 he built this structure, originally called the Meinecke Block, to house his company's offices. His initials can still be seen in the pediment. The building was later renamed the Fine Arts for its proximity to the Pabst Theater and other cultural institutions.

German-born Charles F. Ringer studied architecture in Germany and arrived in Milwaukee in 1870. The Meinecke Block was one of his largest commissions; the building originally cost $100,000.

34. Pabst Theater
144 East Wells Street
Otto Strack, Milwaukee 1895

In 1871, Swiss immigrant and wealthy businessman Jacob Nunnemacher (1819-1876) constructed an elegant opera house and German cafe on this site. Nunnemacher's Opera House, a three-story Italianate building, was purchased by Frederick Pabst. In February 1895, the western two-thirds of the building burned to the ground. The

cafe was spared. Pabst, touring Europe at the time, was told of the tragedy and is said to have wired the instructions, "Rebuild immediately."

Otto Strack was commissioned to design a theater more lavish than the original. On November 9, 1895, only six months after groundbreaking, the Pabst Theater opened its doors. The remaining cafe was incorporated into the design of the new theater but was destroyed by fire in the 1930's.

The exterior of this German Baroque edifice is gray sandstone and orange brick trimmed with metal and terracotta ornament. A decorative iron porch is located on the front facade. Topping the pediment above the main entrance are a gilded lyre and two urns, symbols of music and plenty.

The Pabst Theater seats almost 1,400, and the orchestra pit seats 40 musicians. The interior is profusely decorated with gilded statues, intricate carvings, a lavish staircase, and plush carpeting. A one-ton chandelier, 16 feet long and 12 feet in diameter, with 2,750 feet of crystal strands, hangs in the auditorium. Original balcony seats, made of cast iron with the name Pabst on their backs, remain.

In 1976, the entire theater was restored to its original appearance. In 1989, an elegant corridor was constructed linking the Milwaukee Center's offices, hotel, and theaters to the Pabst.

35. Milwaukee Repertory Powerhouse Theater
Milwaukee Center
108 East Wells Street
Herman J. Esser, Milwaukee   1898
Beckley/Meyers/Flad Architects, Milwaukee   1989

A former power plant provides the shell for this innovative theater. The Renaissance-inspired building was erected by the Milwaukee Electric Railway & Light Company (now Wisconsin Electric Power Company) to supply electricity to downtown customers. The renovation of the masonry and steel building for cultural purposes is an excellent example of urban adaptive re-use.

The 720-seat theater sits comfortably inside the confines of the old electric generator building. Patrons enter via glass-enclosed bridges that pierce the arched openings of its east walls. Located in an annex to the north are support spaces including scenery construction, paint, properties, costume shops, dressing rooms, rehearsal halls, and offices. The Powerhouse Theater is a component of the Milwaukee Center theater complex.

36. Milwaukee Center
111 East Kilbourn Avenue
Skidmore, Owings and Merrill, Houston office   1989

The Milwaukee Center, a 28-story office tower, is the major component of a $100 million business and entertainment complex. A dramatic skylit rotunda, 80 feet high and 110 feet in diameter, is the hub of the development and connects arcades leading to the Pabst Theater, the Milwaukee Repertory's Powerhouse Theater, a cabaret theater, box offices, tenant space, and the 11-story, 200-room Wyndham Hotel.

The Milwaukee Center office tower rises rocket-like to a copper-clad, pyramidal top, which is lighted at night. The tower consists of three diamond-shaped shafts, one atop the other, each turned at a 45-degree angle to the one below. Dressed with red brick, the skyscraper is trimmed with cream-colored limestone and has bronze-

tinted windows. Its design was intended to complement
the nearby Milwaukee City Hall, a century-old landmark. A
pleasant riverwalk extends the length of the whole complex.

37. Milwaukee City Hall

200 East Wells Street
H. C. Koch and Company, Milwaukee   1895

City Hall is perhaps Milwaukee's most significant building. The architecture of the Flemish Renaissance, especially Dutch and Belgian guild halls, inspired the design of this prominent landmark.

Upon its completion, City Hall, with its 350-foot tower, was the third tallest building in America; it was exceeded only by the Philadelphia City Hall (548 feet) and New York City's Pulitzer Building (375 feet). At the time, City Hall was the biggest and most expensive office building in Milwaukee. For more than seven decades it was this city's tallest building. The Firstar Center (601 feet) took the title in 1973.

This block-long, wedge-shaped building is actually a steel and iron-framed cage, with a glass skylight covering a central light court. At base level, the building's dimensions are 105 feet on East Kilbourn Avenue, 330 and 316 feet on its east and west sides respectively, and 56 feet on the East Wells Street front. Because of marshy ground the foundation rests on 25,000 wooden support piles. The building contains nine floors of offices, meeting chambers, and public rooms, all of which open onto corridors that ring the light court.

The exterior is faced with orange brick and granite and embellished with terra-cotta and stone wolf heads, winged dragons, eagles, and carvings of more than 100 infants and cherubs. The massive, foursquare tower has offices on its lower floors. The upper portion is a bell and clock tower, with arched openings marking the belfry. Inside is a ten-ton bell. Containing a 500-pound clapper, the bell has reputedly been heard as far as 24 miles away. The copper-domed turrets, resembling cone-topped beer steins, and four giant clocks set into an elaborate framework of brick and stone are illuminated nightly.

Hundreds of copper plates were riveted together over an iron framework to create the spire atop the tower. This method was similar to that used in the construction of the Statue of Liberty, completed just nine years earlier. An observatory, marked by a balustrade and columns, is reached by a winding staircase through the spire. A bullet-shaped cupola, supporting a 40-foot flagpole with a three-foot-diameter ball, tops the spire.

The million-dollar pricetag caused a local controversy during construction, although the finished building became immediately popular, verifying architect Daniel H. Burnham's comment that "the attainment of harmony, good order, and beauty is not a question of money cost, for in the end good buildings are far cheaper than bad buildings."

38. Performing Arts Center

929 North Water Street
Harry Weese & Associates, Chicago   1969

This contemporary landmark is the home of groups such as the Milwaukee Symphony Orchestra, the Florentine Opera Company, the Milwaukee Ballet, and the Bel Canto Chorus. Inside are theaters, recital halls, banquet rooms, rehearsal space, offices, and storage and ticket areas. The Performing Arts Center's largest public space is Uihlein Hall, which seats 2,300; the intimate Todd Wehr Theater seats 500.

The Performing Arts Center was originally clad with Italian travertine stone. After only twenty years, the original stone was found to be cracking and pulling away from the metal supports that hold it to the building. Although travertine is beautiful, it is very porous. Through years of expansion and contraction, many of the stone panels had bowed noticeably.

Milwaukee architect Charles M. Engberg was called to remedy this situation. He replaced the travertine with a slightly darker Biezanz limestone.

In addition to the exterior recladding, interior changes are also being planned. These include enlarging lobby and entrance areas and renovating concert halls. Completion is scheduled for 1996.

39. River Houses Condominiums
1101-1143 North Edison Street
William Wenzler & Associates, Milwaukee   1985

River Houses Condominiums is a unique residential development in Milwaukee—downtown living with a personal, 30-foot marina slip. These 22 deluxe condominiums line the east bank of the Milwaukee River just south of the Juneau Street Bridge. Each is two stories tall, has 1,500 square feet of living space, and boasts a sunken living room with a wood-burning fireplace. Decks and balconies afford splendid views of the river and skyline.

40. MGIC Plaza
250 East Kilbourn Avenue
Skidmore, Owings and Merrill, Chicago
Fitzhugh Scott Architects, Milwaukee   1972

The Mortgage Guaranty Insurance Corporation built this stunning modernist office complex as its headquarters. A four-story structure anchors one corner of the 2-1/2 acre site. Each floor is cantilevered 15 feet beyond the floor below; the top floor is cantilevered 45 feet over the plaza below. The walls, tightly wrapped with glistening white travertine stone and glass, emphasize the crisp corners. A brisk display of geometries and reflections is the result.

The other office building in this complex, a ten-story rectangle, is finished in the same materials as the four-story building. Together the two structures contain 250,000 square feet of office space. They are connected by a second-story glass skywalk.

A monumental bronze abstract sculpture, 28 feet tall and weighing 12 tons, stands on the south half of the plaza between the two buildings. It was designed and executed in Argentina by artist Alicia Penalba and is entitled *Le Grand Double.* The organic free-flowing lines of the sculpture contrast with the geometric lines of the two buildings.

Le Grand Double
Alicia Penalba
MGIC Plaza

41. 1000 North Water Building

1000 North Water Street
Harwood K. Smith & Partners, Dallas   1991

This building is one of Milwaukee's premier examples of postmodern architecture. Its pink-hued glass facades bow outward under columns and a modified Palladian arch. The tower is capped by a massive copper-clad mansard roof. The skyscraper consists of an eight-story parking facility topped by 16 office floors that provide 300,000 square feet of office space.

One of Milwaukee's most prominent law firms occupies the top floors. Like the 100 East Wisconsin office tower, 1000 North Water also has a law library tucked inside its elaborate roof.

The impressive lobby of 1000 North Water is some 40 feet high. Rich red-orange marble arches mark the elevator lobby, and there is a decorative, multicolored marble floor.

42. Grace Lutheran Church

1209 North Broadway
Armand Koch, Milwaukee   1900

This brick church draws its inspiration from the German Gothic, presenting a stout northern German appearance, complete with characteristic rose window, lancet arches, and finials. The church is cruciform in plan, with a fleche (a small steeple) marking the crossing. A compound-arched, three-portal entrance, framed by terra-cotta decorations, contributes to the Gothic feeling of the building. This church appears earth-bound; it lacks the strong verticality and airiness of other types of Gothic structures. Offsetting this stolid quality are two square towers of unequal height, each supporting octagonal spires.

Due to deterioration of the framework, the top of each tower had to be rebuilt in 1955, producing today's simpler structures.

The church is faced with orange-brown pressed brick accented with similarly colored terra-cotta trim. Encircling the rose window is an inscription referring to the founding of the German congregation:

1850 Evangelisch-Lutherische Gnaden Kirche 1900.

The year 1850 refers to the completion date of a wooden church that formerly occupied this site, while 1900 is the year the present church building was completed.

Architect Armand Koch (1870-1931) was the son of well-known Milwaukee architect Henry C. Koch.

43. Bank One Service Center
1000 North Market Street
Eschweiler & Eschweiler, Milwaukee   1946

This sleek structure was constructed as the bottling house for the nearby Blatz Brewing Company. In 1981, it was gutted and remodeled for offices of the Pabst Brewing Company. Today it serves as an office and computer center for Bank One.

The building's overall composition—asymmetrical

massing, horizontal profile, flat roof, railing-girded set-backs, glass block walls, and ribbon windows—make this a stunning example of the International style applied to an industrial building. The crisp, smooth exterior is glazed, cream-colored brick. Its design echoes the imagery of the machinery, conveyor belts, and bottle washing and auto-mated filling machines once housed within.

44. Blatz Brewery Headquarters Building
1120 North Broadway
Herman Schnetzky, Milwaukee   1890

Valentin Blatz (1826-1894), one of Milwaukee's first and most successful brewers, was born in Bavaria. He set-

tled in Milwaukee in 1848 and was hired as a foreman by Johan Braun, owner of the City Brewery. Upon Braun's death in 1851, Blatz married his widow and changed the brewery's name to his own.

Until Valentin Blatz started to put beer in bottles in 1875, beer was sold only in kegs. Business boomed and soon the brewery had dozens of buildings spread over twenty acres.

Blatz also invested in commercial real estate, was president of the Second Ward Savings Bank (1866-1894), and was a Milwaukee alderman (1872-1873).

Schnetzky's creation is a superb example of Romanesque Revival architecture. Its rock-faced limestone walls express longevity and durability; it appears indestructible. The front elevation is a rich composition of arches, columns, decorative brickwork, and terra cotta.

Pairs of polished granite columns frame the arched entrance to a central pavilion. Near the top of the pavilion is the brewery's trademark, a carved six-pointed stone star that surrounds a hop bud and Valentin Blatz's initials.

Blatz Brewery closed in the 1960s. Office space for a nearby private school now occupies what were once the hushed confines of Valentin Blatz and other brewery executives.

45. Blatz Brewery Residences

1101 North Broadway
Louis Lehle, August Gunzmann, Milwaukee   1891
Shepard Legan Aldrian, Milwaukee
Herbst Eppstein Keller & Chadek Inc., Milwaukee   1988

The landmark Blatz Brewery once consisted of dozens of buildings, including the brew, boiler, wash, and mill houses, and refrigeration, storage, and office buildings. They were linked by brick streets and were designed in an architectural style best described as Industrial Romanesque. Built of Cream City brick and limestone, they were trimmed with copper and terra cotta. The most noteworthy buildings were converted to new uses.

Three brewery stock houses facing North Broadway, East Juneau Avenue, and East Highland Boulevard were converted into 128 luxury apartments, featuring 45 different floor plans.

46. German-English Academy

1020 North Broadway
Crane & Barkhausen, Milwaukee
south half, 1891   north half, 1892

Now an office building, this structure was originally erected as a German-language educational academy, a nineteenth-century private school established to perpetuate German arts, literature, history, and language.

The German-English Academy stands four stories tall on a sandstone foundation. The eclectic architectural style draws from Queen Anne and Romanesque sources. Walls are load-bearing, and inside, wooden posts and beams joined by iron brackets and tie rods also provide structural support. Facades, of Cream City brick, are extensively embellished with yellow-tan terra-cotta decoration. The building originally had a gymnasium marked on the exterior by three two-story-high arched windows. Terra-cotta spandrels here depict a variety of sporting equipment.

47. Plaza East
330 East Kilbourn Avenue
Helmut Jahn, Chicago 1984

Plaza East contains Milwaukee's first postmodern skyscrapers. Both Plaza East towers are six-sided and rise fourteen floors, their front facades angled to the street. The exteriors are composed of 48 percent white pre-formed concrete and 52 percent tinted glass. Steel window mullions are painted a bright red-orange. Atop each tower, a Palladianesque "window" conceals the building's mechanical systems.

Connecting the high-rises is a two-story, 27,000-square-foot atrium called the Crystal Colonnade. Its glass and steel barrel-vaulted roof covers a retail and restaurant space inspired by the interiors of nineteenth-century European public buildings. The Colonnade features a multitude of colors, materials, and Neo-Renaissance forms.

Helmut Jahn was born in Germany and educated in Munich and at the Illinois Institute of Technology. He is best known for designing the State of Illinois Center (1985) in downtown Chicago.

48. St. Mary's Roman Catholic Church

844 North Broadway
Victor Schulte, Milwaukee   1847

Construction of St. Mary's began only two and a half months after Milwaukee was chartered as a city. The cornerstone was laid on April 18, 1846, and the work was completed one year later. It was the city's first German Roman Catholic church and today is its oldest church.

St. Mary's is an example of Zopstil, the German equivalent of the American Federal style. Built of Cream City brick and trimmed in sandstone, this uncluttered structure owes its present appearance to an 1867 remodeling that altered much of the front facade and added an eight-sided tower and steeple.

A plaque on the face of St. Mary's reads:
ECCE ENIM EX HOC BEATAM ME
DICENT OMNES GENERATIONES. LUC 1:48
(For behold, henceforth all generations will
call me blessed. - Luke 1:48.)

49. St. John's Roman Catholic Cathedral

802 North Jackson Street
Victor Schulte, James Douglas, Milwaukee   1847
George Bowman Ferry, Milwaukee   1892

St. John's can be thought of as a two-part composition: an austerely designed church building and a Neo-Baroque bell tower. The main body of the structure is a fine example of the somewhat obscure German Zopstil architecture, a style resembling the American Federal movement of the early nineteenth century. The cathedral is a classically inspired, straightforward design with pedimented stained-glass windows, statuary niches, and brick pilasters.

In 1892, the original tower, weakened with age, was dismantled and replaced with the present German Baroque bell/clock tower. The lowest of the tower's three vertical sections is part of the original building. The top two sections, grafted onto the original tower, feature brick Corinthian columns, copper urns, dome, and lantern.

In 1935, a fire destroyed the interior of the cathedral as well as portions of the east wall. Pittsburgh architect William R. Perry completely redesigned the interior, incorporating a barrel-vaulted nave, colossal arcades separating the nave from the side aisles, an extended chancel area, and a giant baldachino over the altar. New stained-glass windows were also installed.

50. Yankee Hill Apartments
626 East Kilbourn Avenue
Kahler Slater Architects, Milwaukee   1987

Yankee Hill Apartments includes 170 luxury apartments housed in two towers, one 23 stories, the other 19 stories, surrounded by 44 two-story townhouses. Underground parking, an outdoor pool, and many other amenities are available to tenants. The towers' distinctive green gable roofs, bay windows, and red brick facades add color and interest to this century-old neighborhood once populated by immigrants from the eastern seaboard.

51. Juneau Village Apartments

1000 Block of North Jackson Street
Solomon Cordwell Buenz and Associates, Chicago
1965-1971

Six-hundred-unit Juneau Village is the first large-scale, upper-income housing development in downtown Milwaukee. It consists of three tall apartment towers—one 27 stories, the other two 14 stories—and a shopping center. Facades are composed of concrete piers and spandrels, and large panes of glass. The development stands upon a landscaped site with underground parking.

Juneau Village, which recalls the Brutalist designs of post-World War II England and France, is based on the ideas of famous Swiss/French architect and theorist Le Corbusier (1887-1965). One of his philosophies included rebuilding the world's cities by housing people in freestanding, high-rise towers. Buildings would be monochromatic, unornamented, and flat-topped, employ free-standing structural columns at their bases, and incorporate parking. Landscaping and concrete plazas figured prominently into Le Corbusier's idiom. Nearby service-commercial zones would serve the tenants. This design philosophy has been vigorously explored at Juneau Village.

52. Matthew Keenan Townhouse

777 North Jefferson Street
Edward Townsend Mix, Milwaukee 1860
Miller Meier Kenyon Cooper, Architects, Milwaukee 1985

The Matthew Keenan Townhouse, one of the finest Italianate residences in the city, is an antebellum landmark. Standing three floors atop a raised basement, this symmetrical, two-family townhouse displays exquisite detailing, including quoins and a pair of curved staircases with cast-iron newel posts. Italian Renaissance columns support leaf-and-floral-carved brackets and a fanciful veranda. The Keenan Townhouse is constructed of Cream City brick and trimmed with limestone.

Matthew Keenan was a wealthy businessman and politician. In 1852, he was elected clerk of circuit court and went on to become city tax commissioner, alderman, and state legislator. Eventually he became vice president of Northwestern Mutual Life Insurance Company.

In 1984, a fire ruined much of the building, destroying the entire interior and the back and side walls. The front facade was intact, but smoke-damaged. In 1985, the building was totally rebuilt and the inside renovated; the Jefferson Street elevation was restored to its original appearance. The building is currently home to fashionable retail shops and an art gallery.

53. William A. Weber House

785 North Jefferson Street
Architect unknown   1858

The antebellum William A. Weber House is a valuable example of urban residential, Greek Revival architecture. It has an asymmetrical flat front, low-pitched roof, and a Doric portico. Rising two stories plus attic, it is faced with Cream City brick and is accented by a wood cornice. Early photographs reveal that there once were a balustrade immediately above the cornice and a widow's walk atop the deck roof.

William A. Weber (1818-1884) is listed in early city directories as a billiard table manufacturer. The home immediately north of the Weber House at 787 North Jefferson was also built by Weber at about the same time. Currently, these two buildings provide retail and office space.

54. Office On The Square
Shops On Jefferson Street
770-788 North Jefferson Street
Jordan Miller, Milwaukee 1975

This nine-story office and retail complex contains over 100,000 square feet of rentable space. Facades are brown-orange brick with bronze-tinted windows, and exposed steel panels that have been allowed to oxidize to a rich purple color. The sunken courtyard and sensitive scale make this a handsome addition to the Yankee Hill neighborhood.

55. Henry A. Manschott House

718 East Wells Street
Architect unknown   1855

Finding a house this old on downtown's east side is remarkable indeed—it has eluded the wrecker's ball for over a century. The Italianate Manschott House is a fine example of a residential style popular during the nineteenth century. The flat-fronted building has arched windows, complete with window hoods, large brick quoins, and an imposing bracketed cornice. During the 1920s, this Cream City brick building was the home of Francis McGovern (1866-1946), who served two terms as Wisconsin's governor (1911-1915).

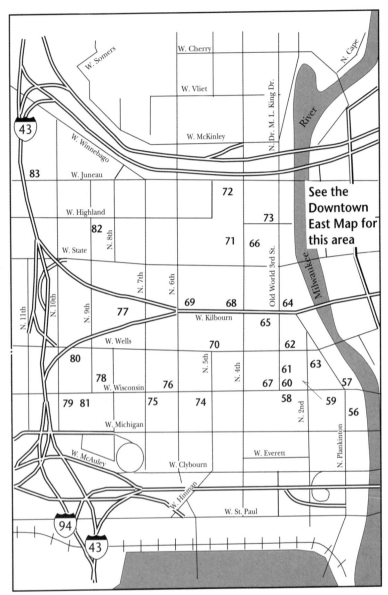

Downtown West

The area downtown and west of the Milwaukee River was once known as Kilbourntown. It was settled by pioneer surveyor Byron Kilbourn, who in 1834 built a cabin on what is now the southwest corner of Third Street and Juneau Avenue. Kilbourn began platting streets and parcels of land and selling real estate west of the river, despite the fact that some of it was beneath a wild rice swamp. Settlers arrived, first by the dozens, then by the hundreds. Kilbourntown grew rapidly, as did Kilbourn's rival development, Solomon Juneau's Juneautown, east of the Milwaukee River.

By 1841, the first brick store in either community was completed by John Hustis on the northwest corner of Third Street and Juneau Avenue, close to Kilbourn's cabin. The Hustis Block stood three stories, measured 40 by 50 feet, and housed Milwaukee's first theater. Kilbourn was especially pleased that it was constructed in Kilbourntown, not on rival turf east of the river. Within a few years, there would be disputes over the locations of river bridges, significant business buildings, and Milwaukee's City Hall.

The Hustis Block was demolished in 1876, the same year that the Nicholas Senn Block was constructed at that location. The Senn Block still stands, only the second building to occupy that site in over 150 years! Hustis went on to found Hustisford, some 45 miles northwest of his famous brick building.

At the turn of the century, West Wisconsin Avenue was known as Grand Avenue. The street was lined with department stores, theaters, hotels, restaurants, and beer gardens; it was Milwaukee's retail and entertainment center. The area was also a government, cultural and media hub. Milwaukee's two largest daily newspapers were founded east of the Milwaukee River, but they eventually migrated west of it. Milwaukee's old Court House on Cathedral Square (east) was demolished when a new courthouse was constructed west of the river on Ninth Street. When a new central library and museum were contemplated in 1893, a west side site was chosen.

Today the western half of downtown Milwaukee is home to the Civic Center (a grouping of seven public buildings), MECCA, the Bradley Center, a new federal building, and the impressive and historic Grand Avenue Retail Center. In addition, the area contains skyscraper hotels and offices, the train station, the giant post office, a technical college, and one of the largest breweries in the country. Covering these approximately 50 blocks are important buildings, structures steeped in history. Where once there were marshes there are now urban landmarks.

Downtown West Buildings

56. Marshall Field & Company
101 West Wisconsin Avenue
Daniel H. Burnham & Co., Chicago
Herman J. Esser, Milwaukee   1902-1925

For many generations this building was known as Gimbels. The "Gimbel Bros. Store" began in 1887 in a building that fronted on Wisconsin Avenue. The business expanded, and soon Gimbels owned all the property on this block. By occupying adjacent buildings and constructing others over a twenty-year period, Gimbels created a single building. By the mid-twenties, Gimbels encompassed 350,000 square feet, nearly thirty times the floor space of the original building. This retailing center was a pioneer in customer comfort, the first Milwaukee store to install escalators, electric elevators, and air conditioning.

The seven-story building is an unusual blend of architectural styles. The north half can be described as Classic Revival, while the south half is a handsome example of Chicago Commercial. The 420-foot riverfront facade of the north half, designed by Herman J. Esser, displays thirteen 50-foot Ionic columns. Its exterior is faced with white glazed brick and terra cotta.

Facing Michigan Street on the south is a facade with little ornamentation and large window bays. Noted architect Daniel H. Burnham (1846-1912) drew the plans for this southern, "modern" portion of the complex. Burnham and his office were also responsible for such famous structures as Chicago's Rookery (1887) and Monadnock (1891) buildings, and Manhattan's Flatiron Building (1902). In the mid-1980s, Marshall Field & Company purchased Gimbels and took over the entire complex.

57. Empire Building
710 North Plankinton Avenue
Kirchoff & Rose, Milwaukee   1927

The thirteen-story Empire Building is one of Milwaukee's most visible Roaring Twenties skyscrapers. In a skillful and typically urban response to its site, the tower occupies the block bounded by Wisconsin and Plankinton avenues and fronts directly on the Milwaukee River. The first two floors are faced with a cream-colored stone, while the floors above are tan brick. Decorative terra-cotta panels adorn the twelfth and thirteenth floors.

The Empire Building houses the famous Riverside

Theater, a grandly styled French Baroque performance space that opened April 29, 1928, and seats 2,436. Its vaudeville and stage shows have presented hundreds of legendary stars to Milwaukee audiences.

58. Grand Avenue Retail Center
275 West Wisconsin Avenue
Elbasani, Logan and Severin, Berkeley, CA   1982

Grand Avenue is this city's most cosmopolitan and architecturally important retail center, and a favorite "people place." As a piece of the urban fabric, the Grand Avenue is a premier example of the blending of renovated, landmark buildings and new construction, of public and private cooperation for the benefit of the city. This $70 million development is home to 162 stores on two levels.

The Grand Avenue stretches three blocks, contains 300,000 square feet, and connects two anchor department stores. It has two distinct sections. The eastern half is a block-long, two-story shopping arcade with five floors of offices above. This segment, the Plankinton Arcade, was designed by the firm of Holabird & Roche of Chicago and was completed in 1916. Constructed to resemble a European marketplace or galleria, this arcade is filled with Italian Gothic and Renaissance detailing.

The western half of the Grand Avenue involved infilling retail space between existing office buildings of various vintages and architectural styles. Two skylit levels of retail shops, a Grand Court with fountains, and a third floor of restaurants and cafes make this section a contemporary showplace.

59. Centre Building and Grand Theater
212 West Wisconsin Avenue
Rapp & Rapp, Chicago   1931

Originally known as the Warner Building, this skyscraper rises 12 stories in the heart of downtown Milwaukee's entertainment and commercial sector. It is one of the finest Art Deco-style buildings in the city. The well-proportioned tower is faced with Indiana limestone, its height emphasized by recessed office windows and bronze spandrels. The Wisconsin Avenue elevation is accented by a

dark-veined marble veneer, which rises ziggurat-like from the street level through the fourth floor in true 1930s form.

The Grand Theater, one of Milwaukee's remaining movie palaces, occupies the lower floors of the Centre Building. Originally named the Warner Theater, it was the showcase for Warner Brothers movies in Milwaukee. It opened to great fanfare on May 1, 1931, just as New Yorkers were celebrating the newest addition to Manhattan's skyline, the 102-story Empire State Building.

Still intact is the Warner's eight-sided, nickel-plated ticket booth lavishly covered in Art Deco designs. The theater's three-story lobby is flanked by 20-foot mirrors and is in vintage condition. Lavish Art Deco trimmings include geometric glass chandeliers and a low relief nickel-plated ceiling. Exit signs, sconces, inlaid veneer walls, an enormous staircase, and foyer complete with murals of streamlined goddesses and birds are orchestrated into a masterpiece of Art Deco design.

In contrast, the auditorium is an interpretation of French Baroque. Much of the original architectural style survived a 1973 remodeling, but where one screen entertained one audience, there are now two of each. The auditorium was split horizontally, the balcony floor was extended to the screen and today two movies can be shown simultaneously. Originally, the auditorium seated 2,431; now the lower floor seats 1,100, the upper 980.

The blank east face of the Centre Building provided a wonderful opportunity for one of Milwaukee's largest public murals. World-famous muralist and Wisconsin native Richard Haas designed and executed a monumental *trompe l'oeil*. Facing east is what the Centre Building *might* have looked like, complete with windows both opened and closed. An immense "glass atrium" was placed in the middle and "reflects" parts of downtown Milwaukee as it looked decades ago, complete with now-demolished landmarks.

60. Straus Building

238 West Wisconsin Avenue
Van Ryn & De Gelleke, Milwaukee   1923

The Straus Building is an important link in the development of the skyscraper in Milwaukee. Its Corporate Gothic style follows earlier classical models and predates the modern high-rise style. It is a remnant of those explorative years, a time when historical styles were employed in the search for an appropriate architectural expression for high-rise buildings.

The eleven-story Straus Building is surmounted by a recessed penthouse with a rooftop promenade. Its exterior is accented by Gothic ornamentation in cream-colored terra cotta and by copper-trimmed details at the cornice. The structure's steel skeleton is wrapped by a single-story base, a soaring midsection shaft, and a decorative top.

Inside is a small marble-walled lobby with a coffered, barrel-vaulted ceiling.

German-born Arthur J. Straus became wealthy by dealing in Milwaukee real estate. The Straus Building was his company's headquarters.

Henry J. Van Ryn, born in Milwaukee in 1864, studied architecture under Charles A. Gombert and later worked for notable architects James Douglas and Edward Townsend Mix. Gerrit J. De Gelleke, born in Milwaukee in 1872, formed a partnership with Van Ryn in 1897. Both had Dutch backgrounds and were familiar with Europe's historical styles. The firm designed many public schools, office structures, and campus buildings at the University of Wisconsin-Milwaukee.

61. Wisconsin Hotel
720 North Third Street
Holabird & Roche, Chicago   1913

At the time of its completion, the twelve-story Wisconsin was Milwaukee's tallest hotel. The building is faced with red and white brick, set into a checkerboard pattern. Atop the 500-room Wisconsin a large gable and a pitched roof charmingly recall the architecture of a French chateau.

62. Century Building

808 North Third Street
Alfred S. Alschuler, Chicago   1924

The Century Building is a distinguished high-rise office building. Architect Alfred S. Alschuler (1876-1940) had worked in the office of the talented architect/engineer Dankmar Adler. Adler, of course, was the partner of Louis H. Sullivan, the great Chicago "skyscraper architect" of the nineteenth century. Alschuler's firm designed the London Guarantee Building, one of the most prominent skyscrapers of 1920s Chicago. The 20-story London Guarantee (now Stone Container) and Milwaukee's Century Building are stylistically similar.

The Century Building rises eight stories and is wrapped by white glazed brick and terra cotta. The walls are embellished with Renaissance decorations, such as garland drapings, escutcheons (containing the overlapping letters C and B), fleur-de-lis, vitruvian scroll, and are topped by a balustered parapet. A highly detailed, brass-trimmed main entrance opens into a handsomely appointed L-shaped lobby, with marble walls, a coffered ceiling, Renaissance chandeliers, and etched brass elevator doors with lunettes above.

63. Germania Building

135 West Wells Street
Schnetzky and Liebert, Milwaukee 1896

At its completion, the Germania Building was the tallest (135 feet) and largest office building on Milwaukee's west side, a robust example of a Classic Revival skyscraper with Teutonic overtones. The Germania Building was erected as the headquarters of *Die Germania*, the world's largest German-language newspaper at the time. This profitable enterprise was founded by George Brumder (1839-1910), a German immigrant who recognized the need to keep German-speaking Americans informed of world events. The paper's popularity and financial success necessitated larger quarters by the 1890s, and this "Wagnerian" skyscraper was erected.

Trapezoidal in plan, this eight-story structure displays Doric and Ionic columns, bay windows, arches, cartouches, pediments, statuary, and carved cherubs. Topping the building are five spike-capped copper domes.

The interior of the Germania Building contains marble terrazzo floors and wainscoting, and coffered and delicately carved ceilings. On the exterior, giant carved-stone lions guard the main entrance. Above, a cartouche

inscribed with the letter B pays homage to its newspaper's founder.

A three-ton, ten-foot bronze statue once stood on a plinth above the main entrance. The statue depicted "Die Germania," a female allegorical symbol of the Germanic tribes during the time of Caesar. Anti-German sentiment during World War I prompted its removal.

64. Milwaukee County Historical Society
910 North Third Street
Kirchoff & Rose, Milwaukee   1913

The Second Ward Savings Bank erected this two-story French Renaissance Revival building, replacing an 1866 office on this site. In 1928, the bank was absorbed into the First Wisconsin National Bank (now Firstar), and the building continued as a bank until 1966, when it was donated to Milwaukee County.

The exterior is of Indiana limestone. Its elegant facades are adorned with fluted Ionic columns, Beaux-Arts-styled arched windows, and carved decorations. Inside are exhibits about Milwaukee history and a research library.

65. Hyatt-Regency Hotel

333 West Kilbourn Avenue
Py-Vavra Architects, Milwaukee 1980

The Hyatt-Regency Hotel rises 18 floors and contains restaurants, lounges, convention facilities, and 500 guest rooms. The skeleton is poured-in-place concrete; exterior walls consist of concrete panels and dark bronze-tinted windows.

Inside, Milwaukee's tallest and largest atrium rises 17 floors. Guest rooms open onto corridors that ring the atrium. An abstract metal sculpture, suspended from the atrium's ceiling, was designed by world-famous New York artist Richard Lippold (born Milwaukee, 1920). Titled *Wings Of Welcome*, it is 85 feet tall and weighs one-half ton. Four glass-enclosed "elevator capsules" glide upward to guest floors and a rooftop restaurant and lounge called Polaris, which rotates once per hour and affords patrons a panoramic view of the city.

With Polaris revolving on top, the Hyatt is easily identifiable on the Milwaukee skyline.

66. Turner Hall

1034 North Fourth Street

H. C. Koch and Company, Milwaukee   1883

Designed in a simple Romanesque style wrapped by Cream City brick, this three-story clubhouse rests upon a sandstone base and is topped by a square belvedere with a pyramidal cap. In an interesting color contrast, a deep red brick trims the arched windows of the main facade.

Turner Hall was built by a German organization called the *Sozialer Turnverein* ("Turner" for short). The building, still housing the Turner organization, contains a large restaurant, dance hall, meeting rooms, and a gymnasium. The Turners advocate intellectualism and promote music, theater, politics, literature, and physical fitness.

Unfortunately Turner Hall has undergone major modifications over the years. The main entrance has been greatly altered, as have the window openings and portions of the interior. A careful restoration could undo the damage inflicted over the years.

67. Henry S. Reuss Federal Plaza
310 West Wisconsin Avenue
Perkins & Will, Chicago   1983

The Reuss Federal Plaza rises 14 floors and contains 700,000 square feet of office space. Though built by a private developer, the major tenant is the federal government, with some 40 agencies employing 1,500 people. It is the central node in the second-story skywalk system that links major downtown buildings.

The building is composed of two halves separated by a dramatic atrium that rises 175 feet to a glass skylight. The western, cube-shaped half contains office space for the federal government, while the eastern, wedge-shaped half houses private tenants. This 200-foot-long central space is crossed by "sky-bridges" at floors 4, 7, 10, and 13.

The exterior of the Reuss Federal Plaza is composed of broad horizontal bands of opaque, fade-resistant, cobalt-blue panels alternating with rows of silver-toned, reflective windows. The deep blue color was controversial, but it does inject a needed interest into a blandly colored neighborhood.

The building design allowed for a generous plaza at the southeast corner of the site. The plaza's centerpiece is

a five-piece, 70-ton, Norwegian blue granite sculpture. Artist Helaine Blumenfeld polished the sensuously curved stone to glass-like smoothness, a perfect counterpoint to the rigid steel geometries and reflective glass of the building behind.

68. Milwaukee Arena
420 West Kilbourn Avenue
Eschweiler & Eschweiler, Milwaukee   1950

Before the completion of the nearby Bradley Center, this noble building was the home of the Milwaukee Bucks basketball team and the Milwaukee Admirals hockey team. It can accommodate 15,000 spectators and is still host to circuses, trade shows, rallies, concerts, and pageants. The Milwaukee Arena is faced with red brick and is topped with a copper-clad, concentric-arched roof that rises 110 feet.

69. Milwaukee Auditorium
500 West Kilbourn Avenue
Ferry & Clas, Milwaukee   1909

Vaguely Classic Revival in appearance (the rear elevations have Classical pilasters and pediments), this brick-faced building has been a center of public events since its opening on September 21, 1909. Inside are meeting rooms, convention halls, and exhibit areas. The main exhibit hall, which seats 6,250, measures 225 feet long, 100 feet wide, and 65 feet high. It is still used for conventions, rallies, concerts and other public functions.

The Milwaukee Auditorium was built as a replacement for the giant Milwaukee Industrial Exposition Building. That flamboyant Victorian building, designed by Milwaukee architect Edward Townsend Mix, opened in 1881. It was a multitowered, block-wide, steel, glass, and brick extravaganza measuring 400 by 300 feet. A 200-foot, eight-sided dome with a public observatory, topped the building. On the afternoon of June 4, 1905, it was struck by lightning and burned to the ground. Four years later the more restrained Milwaukee Auditorium was completed on the same site.

70. MECCA
Milwaukee Exposition
& Convention Center & Arena

West Kilbourn Avenue and North Fifth Street
Welton Becket & Associates, Chicago   1974

Occupying a 5.5-acre site, MECCA provides convention, trade show, and exposition facilities for virtually all of Milwaukee's major conventions and meetings. It was built by the city for $15 million to bring Milwaukee into the "big leagues" of the profitable convention business.

MECCA is two stories tall, contains 400,000 square feet, and can accommodate up to 15,000 people—or nearly 34,000 when combined with the Auditorium and Arena. The main exhibit space, the 66,000-square-foot Great Hall, is flanked by two other halls each containing 33,000 square feet. The second floor contains 24 meeting rooms and a large three-tiered cocktail lounge overlooking the Great Hall. MECCA's kitchens can produce meals for up to 6,500. The second level is connected to Milwaukee's skywalk system, enabling visitors to stroll through downtown in climate controlled comfort.

The fully air-conditioned structure contains more than one million bricks and 250,000 concrete blocks, and is supported by some 2,000 pilings. The exterior of the first floor is composed of dark brown brick; the second floor, cantilevered above, is faced with pale white steel sheathing.

71. Bradley Center
1001 North Fourth Street
Hellmuth, Obata & Kassabaum, Kansas City
Zimmerman Design Group, Milwaukee
Kahler Slater Torphy Engberg, Milwaukee   1988

With a seating capacity of 20,000, the Bradley Center is one of the largest, most visited buildings in Milwaukee. It is home to Milwaukee's professional basketball and hockey teams, the Bucks and the Admirals.

Faced with over 110,000 square feet of rose-colored carnelian granite, it is topped with a sloping domed roof covered with leaded copper. Two atriums, one facing east and one facing west, both walled with black glass, mark the public entrances. There are 14 ticket windows, 16 escalators, two passenger elevators, and 110 television monitors (one in each concession stand and private suite). The giant building is supported by 1,500 tons of structural steel and rises 154 feet (the equivalent of a 14-story building).

This sports and entertainment facility honors Milwaukee industrialist Harry Lynde Bradley, co-founder of the Allen-Bradley Company (see building #88). It was a gift to the community from Bradley's daughter, Jane Pettit, and her husband, Lloyd. References to the factory Harry Lynde Bradley founded are subtlely employed in the Center's design. Octagons figure prominently: in plan it is eight-sided (325 feet wide by 445 feet long), and on its exterior are large octagonal air vents, which recall the eight-sided clocks that tower over the company's head-quarters building.

72. Union Brewery Building
423 West Juneau Avenue
architect unknown   1853

Built when Franklin Pierce was President and Milwaukee was only seven years old, this Federal style building is one of the oldest in downtown Milwaukee. The style is characterized by its cubic shape, absence of decoration, stepped parapet end walls, and plain brick construction. Because Milwaukee was so young, the Federal style here spanned only the years 1840 to 1860. In older cities, buildings of this type were erected as early as 1785.

In 1843, David Gipfel built one of Milwaukee's first breweries on this site. Upon his death in 1849, his son Charles took charge, named the enterprise the Union Brewery, and built this new brewery.

Consisting of three stories plus an attic, the Union

Brewery was constructed of Cream City brick and wooden timbers. The original building measured 36 feet wide by 26 feet deep; a two-story rear addition was constructed later.

Repositioning windows and entrances, reconfiguring the interiors, and general neglect have unfortunately left this building in need of renovation. Nevertheless, the Union Brewery Building transcends its condition and emerges as a solid example of the austere Federal genre.

73. Lipps Block
1101 North Third Street
Charles A. Gombert, Milwaukee   1878

German immigrant John Lipps established a millinery business in Milwaukee in 1858 and commissioned this building to house his firm. With the exception of its first-floor exterior, this eclectic Victorian structure has retained much of its original appearance.

The Lipps Block, three floors plus attic, is faced with sandstone panels and Cream City brick. A stone corbel course, terra-cotta accents, and a bracketed sheet-metal cornice add charm to this antique structure.

74. Marc Plaza Hotel

509 West Wisconsin Avenue
Holabird & Roche, Chicago   1927

At 24 stories, this is Wisconsin's tallest hotel. The Marc Plaza was Milwaukee's first modern skyscraper to employ setbacks—the top floors are smaller than the lower floors. Viewed from the east or west, the 600-room hotel resembles a large throne. The first five floors of the exterior are faced with limestone and adorned with low-relief Art Deco carvings of foliate patterns, peacocks, and female nudes. The remainder of the building is faced with red brick.

The lobby is lavishly decorated in French Baroque style. Crystal chandeliers and beautifully ornamented ceilings, walls, and staircases make this one of the more elegant spaces in the city.

Built by Milwaukee businessman Walter Schroeder (1878-1967), this hotel was originally known as the Schroeder. It contained 811 guest rooms, but a remodeling in 1973 reduced the number of rooms while increasing the number of suites on the top five floors. In 1972, Milwaukee's Marcus Corporation purchased the Schroeder and the name was changed to reflect its new ownership.

A rooftop sign, one of the largest in Wisconsin, spells out the hotel's name in 16-foot letters which glow red at night. The building is topped by a 340-foot steel mast, which supports a 51-foot television transmitting antenna.

75. 633 Building
633 West Wisconsin Avenue
Robert Lee Hall & Associates, Memphis   1962

The 633 Building rises 20 floors and contains a large intercity bus station, multilevel parking deck, and 400,000 square feet of office space. Originally built as the headquarters for the Clark Oil and Refining Company, this skyscraper is a fine example of 1960s modernism. Panels of marble aggregate, then a new building material, are used on exterior walls. Floors rise undifferentiated to a flat unadorned top. Setbacks and decorative ornamentation were eschewed for the repetitive and reductivist look favored then by corporate America.

Atop a raised platform on the roof is one of Milwaukee's most visible signs. The 50-by-50-foot illuminated sign

revolves every 40 seconds and advertises various products and local events.

76. Wisconsin Tower
606 West Wisconsin Avenue
Weary & Alford, Chicago   1930

The 21-story Wisconsin Tower, Milwaukee's second-tallest stone-faced building (tallest is NML Data Center, #6), is an excellent example of Art Deco architecture, featuring finely proportioned setbacks and geometric detailing. The base of the Wisconsin Tower is faced with pink and black marble; the upper floors are sheathed in Indiana limestone. Metal spandrels and grillwork, depicting stylized birds and floral patterns, encircle the building.

The building's base measures 70 by 150 feet, with the tower tapering to 68 feet square at the top, 250 feet above Wisconsin Avenue. Topping the building is a large steel mast in Art Deco style; bracketed to the mast is a

communications antenna.

Inside, the lobby walls are marble. Art Deco designs are executed in the metal trim around the elevators, radiator grills, floor directory, and mailbox. The elevator doors and the inside of each cab are etched with a large schooner within a geometric sunburst. The nautical theme reflects the fact that this skyscraper was first called the Mariner Tower, honoring the tower's builder and major tenant, the Mariner Realty Company, a firm founded by John Mariner (1868-1930) in 1920.

77. Milwaukee County Courthouse
901 North Ninth Street
Albert Randolph Ross, New York City   1931

In 1928, Milwaukee County sponsored a nationwide architectural design competition for a new courthouse. This winning design, which beat out 30 other entries, is a powerful example of Roman neoclassical architecture.

The building is a whopping 730 feet wide, 197 feet deep, and 190 feet tall. Sixty-two Corinthian columns, each 34 feet tall, surround the building. Another six colossal columns each rise 54 feet on the building's east facade. The whole structure is girded by stone owls (these symbols of wisdom each weigh 5,000 pounds), lioness heads, and inscriptions. The courthouse is faced with Bedford limestone.

On the east facade is an inscription: Erected by the People and Dedicated to the Administration of the Law. Elsewhere is a Latin inscription: *Vox Populi Vox Dei* (The voice of the people is the voice of the Gods). Three large, arched doorways facing the Civic Center are each labeled with a different virtue: Truth, Justice, and Order.

The interior is equally impressive, with barrel-vaulted, marble-lined corridors, 32 lavishly appointed courtrooms, and hundreds of offices and public rooms. Though the courthouse rises only eight floors, its 20-foot ceilings make it equivalent to a 15-story building in height.

78. Milwaukee Central Public Library
814 West Wisconsin Avenue
Ferry & Clas, Milwaukee 1897

This monumental three-story building occupies a half block and is faced with Bedford limestone. Its symmetrical front elevation displays lavish French and Italian Renaissance forms. Corinthian columns and pilasters, Palladian window openings, and other detailing are crisply carved and remain in pristine condition.

A large dome rises above the entrance rotunda where an intricate mosaic floor, marble staircases, and a beautiful coffered ceiling recall the splendor of the great buildings of Europe. The library owes much of its appearance to the classical styles espoused by proponents of the

City Beautiful movement and to the lavish buildings at Chicago's World's Columbian Exposition of 1893.

The design of this great institution was chosen after a nationwide competition. Seventy-four entries were received from around the country, including one from a young Frank Lloyd Wright.

79. Calvary Presbyterian Church
935 West Wisconsin Avenue
Henry C. Koch, Milwaukee
Julius Hess, Milwaukee   1870

Calvary Presbyterian Church, an excellent example of Milwaukee's post-Civil War church architecture, draws its inspiration from French Gothic country churches, as evidenced by its strong vertical emphasis, fine proportions, and delicately ornamented profile. The base is sandstone blocks, and the walls are Cream City brick painted red.

Gothic ornamentation includes stepped buttresses, finials, stained glass, and lancet-arched windows.

A large west tower and a more diminutive east tower rise from the north corners of the building. The smaller tower is capped by a copper-clad spire. The larger is surmounted by a slender steeple and soars 210 feet. It is topped not with a cross but with a poppyhead finial.

80. Alexander Mitchell Mansion
900 West Wisconsin Avenue
John Bently, Milwaukee   1855
Edward Townsend Mix, Milwaukee   1873

Businessman and banker Alexander Mitchell (1817-1887) built this two-story Italianate house in 1855. In 1873 the house was enlarged and remodeled from plans by E. T. Mix. These changes drastically altered the original, wrapping the Italianate in French Second Empire clothing, the 1870s design rage of the wealthy.

Constructed of Cream City brick (now painted

white), the Mitchell Mansion has two full stories, plus a third that is encircled by a straight mansard roof. Bay windows, gables, iron cresting, bracketed cornices, and deeply carved trim mark the mansion as a prime example of high-Victorian architecture. The mansion's handsomest element is its four-story tower, complete with an attic tucked into its mansard roof.

After Mitchell's death, the mansion became the headquarters of the Deutscher [German] Club which enlarged and altered it. The organization, renamed the Wisconsin Club during World War I because of anti-German sentiment, still occupies this elaborate home.

81. YMCA Building

915 West Wisconsin Avenue
Grassold, Johnson & Associates, Milwaukee   1954

The YMCA Building is one of Milwaukee's first International style high-rises. Standing 18 stories, this flat-topped, flat-walled building has no reference to historicism, and no applied ornamentation. Exterior materials include stainless steel, glass, and blond brick. An external brick bay rising the full height of the tower marks the loca-

tion of the elevator shafts.

The building's external lettering was the nearest the architects came to applied ornament. The 12-foot-tall letters, in true International style, were clear, plain characters, properly scaled, and conformed to the geometric character of the overall design.

The building contains 480 hotel rooms and facilities for food service and athletic and social events. Now owned by Marquette University, it is used as a dormitory.

82. Trinity Evangelical Lutheran Church
1026 North Ninth Street
Frederick Velguth, Milwaukee   1878

Milwaukee's quintessential nineteenth-century German church, Trinity is a fine example of Victorian Gothic architecture, drawing primarily from German prototypes. It is constructed of Cream City brick with sandstone detailing. Intricate brick designs appear on all facades. Overall

verticality is reinforced by pinnacles, brick buttresses topped by sandstone caps, and two tall towers, one with a 200-foot spire.

The floor plan is the Latin cross. At the crossing of the nave and the transepts is a small spire called a fleche. Flanking the entrance are two stone tablets bearing the completion date and the architect's name.

Inside Trinity, worshipers sit on oak pews and face a delicately and elaborately carved oak altar and raised pulpit, complete with a baldachino. Towering above the choir loft is a large organ with over 1,600 pipes.

83. Pabst Brewery Malt Elevator
1000 Block of West Juneau Avenue
Klug & Smith Engineers, Milwaukee   1953

The malt elevator is 184 feet tall, 98 feet square, and topped by an illuminated, 25-foot-square, revolving Pabst sign. Inside, 25 silos hold 840,000 bushels of malt products, while three others contain more than two million pounds of grits. The elevator's modernist, albeit utilitarian, sculptural form is devoid of any applied decoration. Its white concrete, cylindrical facades, visible for miles, are strong architectural images.

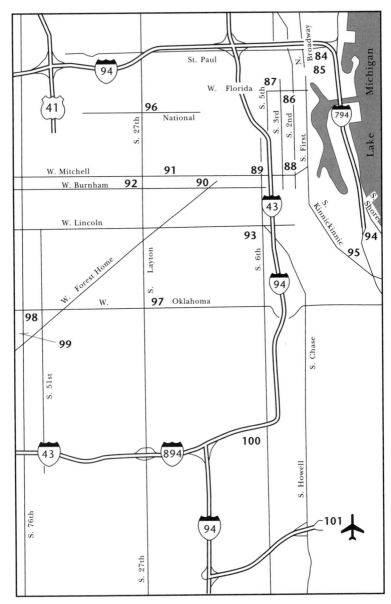

South Side

Chapter Three
South Side

The third pioneer of early Milwaukee, after Solomon Juneau and Byron Kilbourn, was George H. Walker. In 1834, Walker built a cabin and a trading post at present-day First and Seeboth streets, and staked claim to all the land south of Juneau's and Kilbourn's territories. Walker sold the first lot on the south side to Mark Noble, Jr., on June 6, 1836. This lot was about three blocks south of Walker's own cabin, near where the Abel Decker Doublehouse (building #86) stands today.

The first neighborhood south of downtown Milwaukee, appropriately called Walker's Point, is the south side's oldest neighborhood. It is bounded on the north and northeast by the Menomonee and Milwaukee rivers respectively, and on the southeast by the Kinnickinnic River. What was then an area of swampy lowlands was eventually reclaimed. Walker's Point developed into a teeming, working-class enclave of German and Polish immigrants.

Today, Milwaukee's south side is a collection of diverse neighborhoods. Much of the population of 185,000 is of Eastern European descent, especially Polish, Czech, German, and Hungarian. Italians and Hispanics also contribute to the mix. The residents are primarily Roman Catholic. The south side is also home to many factories and other industrial facilities. The architecture of this part of the city is rooted in its European heritage and its industrial base.

Milwaukee's south side is an area of well-kept homes, handsome parks and boulevards, and an impressive array of churches. The Walker's Point neighborhood has many fine examples of Greek Revival, Italianate, and Queen Anne style houses. The Bay View area boasts a yacht club and stunning views of Lake Michigan and downtown Milwaukee from its lakefront bluffs. Sprinkled throughout the south side are many small Victorian commercial buildings and thousands of homes in bungalow, craftsman vernacular, and Cape Cod styles.

South Side Buildings

84. Jewett & Sherman Block
225 East St. Paul Avenue
architect unknown   1875

This building is typical of American factory and warehouse buildings of the late nineteenth century. The four-story structure is faced with Cream City brick, which was cleaned to its original color in 1978, revealing brick patterns hidden for a century under layers of dirt and soot. Interior brick walls and timbers were exposed and cleaned to enhance the structure's new office, retail, and gallery uses.

The Jewett & Sherman Company, a wholesaler dealing in ground coffee, spices, and baking powders, built this 60-by-125-foot Victorian Gothic building as its warehouse and office. It anchors the north end of an area known as Commission Row, Milwaukee's century-old produce center. Proximity to the Milwaukee River and major railroad lines made the neighborhood a focal point of the produce trade, and from here fruits and vegetables were (and still are) dispensed to grocery stores throughout the city.

85. The Buffalo Building

302 North Broadway
Eugene Liebert, Milwaukee 1900

The Buffalo Building is a fine example of sensitive rehabbing, following a national trend of introducing residents to "rediscovered" urban manufacturing buildings and neighborhoods. This is Milwaukee's first such effort.

The building was constructed by Ernst von Baumbach, owner of the Phoenix Hosiery Company, a textile manufacturing firm. Later it was the home of Cohen Brothers, a men's clothing firm.

The Buffalo is a sturdy, five-story brick box on a sandstone base. The facade is composed of orange-tan brick accented by decorative orange terra cotta. A massive cornice with scroll brackets, interspersed by terra-cotta rosettes, encircles the building.

In the early 1980s the Buffalo Building was renovated into office, retail, and condominium space. Thirteen residential units on the top two floors feature exposed wood beams and columns, large windows, hardwood floors, and exposed Cream City brick walls. What was a dingy loading dock and freight elevator has become the condominium lobby with a new passenger elevator.

86. Abel Decker Doublehouse
408-410 South Third Street
Architect unknown   1857

Early Milwaukee settler and grocer Abel Decker (1817-1895) constructed this Federal style doublehouse (two joined residences sharing a party wall). It is one of the few residential examples of this style and type remaining in Milwaukee.

The exterior, which remains intact, was carefully restored by new owners in 1993. The Cream City brick was cleaned, rotted porches were removed, the roof was repaired, and windows were replaced. The two-story units, each 21 feet wide and 32 feet deep, are topped by attic spaces marked by shallow gables and windows that face west over this 160-year-old neighborhood.

87. Ziegler Candy Company Building

402-424 West Florida Street
Herman Schnetzky, Milwaukee   1907

Reported to be the first building in America to use a concrete skeleton, this office, warehouse, and manufacturing structure demonstrated the revolutionary possibilities of this type of construction.

The seven-story Ziegler Building is faced with light brown brick and topped by a tin cornice of classical inspiration. The primary facade is asymmetrically composed and has many large windows.

88. Allen-Bradley Clock Tower

1201 South Second Street
Fitzhugh Scott and Fitzhugh Scott Jr., Milwaukee   1962

One of the most recognizable landmarks in Milwaukee is the Allen-Bradley Clock Tower. Some of the buildings of the Allen-Bradley Company, an electronic equipment and components firm, date from 1919. But it is the tower with its four clocks that identifies the company.

The Allen-Bradley manufacturing plant contains over one million square feet of floor space. Assembly, laboratory, warehouse, and office areas cluster beneath the 280-foot concrete tower. The tower itself is 45 feet square

and houses the company's headquarters and research facilities in addition to the clocks.

The *Guinness Book of World Records* lists the Allen-Bradley clock as the "largest four-faced clock in the world." It is actually four separate clocks. Each of the octagonal clock faces is nearly twice the size of the clocks on London's Big Ben tower (although London's tower at 316 feet is slightly taller than the Allen-Bradley tower). On a clear night, the lighted faces can be seen 40 miles out on Lake Michigan. Clock facts:

- Each clock weighs over twelve tons.
- The face of each clock is 40 feet 3-1/2 inches wide.
- Each hour hand is 15 feet 9 inches long, and weighs 490 pounds.
- Each minute hand is 20 feet long and weighs 530 pounds.
- Hour markings on each face are four feet high.
- Two tons of glass (76 pieces, mainly in four-foot-square sections) cover each clock face.
- The tower is topped by a 36-foot flagpole.
- The clock serves as an official navigation aid and is so designated on the maps of the United States Coast Guard.

89. St. Stanislaus Roman Catholic Church
1681 South Fifth Street
Leon Alfons Schmidtner, Milwaukee   1873
Mark A. Pfaller, Milwaukee   1962

One of Milwaukee's most important landmarks, St. Stanislaus is an excellent example of German Baroque Revival architecture. The church was founded by Polish immigrants in 1866, and its landmark building holds the distinction of having the state's most exterior clocks - eight. It was also the first Polish church built in America.

The building surface is Cream City brick, accented with limestone trim. Facades are embellished with statuary, mosaic tiles, stained-glass windows, and pedimented and arched entrances. On the south facade is a brilliantly colored tile mosaic depicting the Virgin Mary holding the Christ Child. The most visible and impressive elements of St. Stanislaus are its two bell/clock towers. Each 200-foot tower has four clocks and is topped by a gold-plated dome and a lantern.

The church was remodeled and renovated in the early 1960s, when the east facade and the interior were altered. The most conspicuous changes occurred on the tower domes. Original copper cladding was replaced with a surface of 23-karat gold leaf. After gilding in 1962, the domes shone brilliantly, even on an overcast day. Over the last 30 years air pollution dulled the surfaces.

90. Milwaukee Public Library - Forest Home Branch

1432 West Forest Home Avenue
Von Grossmann, Burroughs and Van Lanen Architects, Milwaukee   1966

This building, with its strong sense of clarity and refinement, is an outstanding example of modern architecture, with skillfully manipulated space and use of a minimum number of materials. The design owes much to the influence of master architect Mies Van der Rohe (1886-1969).

The building's skeleton is a grid of vertical and horizontal steel I-beams, which were painted black inside but left to weather to a rich brown color on the outside. Clerestory windows, a wood-joist ceiling, burnt-orange tile floors, black canister lights, and modern furniture accent the interior. Twenty-six textured, precast concrete wall

panels serve as book bays.

The library, which occupies a wedge-shaped site, contains 15,000 square feet of floor space and houses 60,000 books. The American Institute of Steel Construction granted this building the Architectural Award of Excellence "in recognition of outstanding esthetic design in structural steel."

91. St. Vincent de Paul Catholic Church
2114 West Mitchell Street
Bernard Kolpacki, Milwaukee   1900

St. Vincent's, one of the great landmark churches of Milwaukee, is a superb example of German Baroque Revival architecture.

The building is of brown brick trimmed with limestone. Its main facade contains both arched and pedimented entrances. Above the entrances are rose windows and a statuary niche containing the church's namesake. Two impressive bell towers rise over the nave; the eastern and western towers stand 180 feet and 140 feet respectively. Each buttressed tower is topped by a copper dome and lantern. The eastern tower houses a four-faced clock at the top.

92. Arthur L. Richards Houses
2700 Block of West Burnham Street
Frank Lloyd Wright, Spring Green, Wisconsin   1916

This Milwaukee block boasts a row of six homes designed by Frank Lloyd Wright. They are early examples of prefabricated housing units, executed in the Prairie style.

The four western-most buildings are two-story duplexes; the other two are one-story bungalows. Originally all were surfaced with stucco and wood trim, but through the years, alterations occurred, including new siding and enclosed porches. One of the duplexes has been converted to a single-family home. Milwaukee developer Arthur L. Richards built all six of these houses using Wright's American System Built prefab plans of 1911. None were supervised by Wright during construction.

93. Basilica of St. Josaphat
601 West Lincoln Avenue
Erhard Brielmaier, Milwaukee   1901

The Basilica of St. Josaphat is the most significant architectural landmark on Milwaukee's south side, and one of Wisconsin's greatest buildings. One of only 16 basilicas in the United States, it is the city's largest church, seating 2,400.

115

St. Josaphat's, America's first Polish Roman
Catholic basilica, was assembled from 200,000 tons of salvage from Chicago's Federal Building, which was demolished in 1895. Shipped to Milwaukee on 500 flatcars, the
salvage included stone for the exterior walls, six huge
granite columns, doors, hardware, and light fixtures.

The cornerstone was laid on July 4, 1897. Construction was a monumental undertaking; parishioners excavat-
ed the site with picks and shovels, and horses and wagons
hauled earth away and brought construction materials to
the site. Amazingly, only one construction death was
reported. The great church was dedicated on July 21,
1901, and consecrated on November 18, 1928. On March
10, 1929, Pope Pius XI elevated St. Josaphat to the dignity
of a minor basilica.

Based on the design of St. Peter's in Rome, this
structure is a faithful rendition of the Italian Baroque
style. In plan, the basilica is cruciform, 190 feet north to
south, and 127 feet east to west. A giant portico, with
Corinthian columns, marks the building's main entrance.
Two 100-foot belfry towers frame a rose window. Gilded
crosses, a statue of St. Josaphat, Corinthian pilasters, classical carvings, arches, and pediments contribute to the rich
exterior.

The majestic basilica has one of the five largest
domes in the world; it is larger than that of the celebrated
Taj Mahal in India or of Santa Sophia in Istanbul. The

rotunda is octagonal. Eight giant piers support the dome, which rises 250 feet (the height of a 20-story building). Its circumference at the drum, the circular wall that supports the dome, is 240 feet. The dome is covered with copper and weighs over 1,500 tons; on completion, it was the world's only structural steel dome.

The unrivaled interior is profusely decorated with stained-glass windows, statuary, shrines, and a high altar with a baldachino. In 1926, Roman painter Gonippo Raggi completed a series of murals throughout the interior. The nave and transepts are dramatically lighted, and the interior of the lavishly painted dome is breathtaking.

German-born architect Erhard Brielmaier (1841-1917) began practicing in Cincinnati, then moved to Milwaukee in 1874. He became popular, with a reputation for designing churches in all the historical styles.

94. Bay View Terrace Condominiums
2525 South Shore Drive
Rasche, Schroeder & Spransy, Milwaukee   1964

At 25 stories, Bay View Terrace is the tallest building on Milwaukee's south side. It is a noteworthy example

of a 1960s residential high-rise. The building is faced with brick, concrete, stainless steel, and glass.

Because the Bay View Terrace stands on a hill, its residents have unobstructed views of the city, a nearby yacht club, and Lake Michigan. The high-rise is visible for miles and dominates the century-old Milwaukee neighborhood known as Bay View.

95. Milwaukee Public Library - Bay View Branch
2570 South Kinnickinnic Avenue
Engberg Anderson Architects, Milwaukee   1993

The Bay View Library anchors the heart of this century-old Milwaukee neighborhood. It seems out of place and appears noncontextual, but this is one instance where architecture helps to reinvent a neighborhood, forcing a new, more critical look at the surrounding buildings.

The library site is a trapezium (a four-sided plot having no parallel sides), narrow and steeply pitched in spots. Onto this difficult site a one-story, 15,000-square-foot building designed to house 60,000 books was cleverly placed.

The library's boxy saw-tooth design is penetrated by a "wedge piece," creating a most effective and handsome composition. The "wedge" carves out interior space and gracefully enters upon the main browsing room/gallery, which dramatically rises 23 feet. The gallery

terminates at a canted window wall on the south. Above are twelve large laminated wood-and-steel trusses spanning this 29-foot-wide "nave." They support an arched, white metal ceiling. Between the trusses are translucent glass clerestory windows. The floor of the main entry foyer is a linoleum mosaic by artist Peter Flanary depicting three historic map renditions of Bay View.

Primary structural materials are three shades of brick, silver painted steel, tinted glass, and white maple for trim and bookshelves.

96. Mitchell Park Horticultural Conservatory
550 South Layton Boulevard
Donald L. Grieb, Milwaukee   1959-67

These unique "sixties-modern" buildings house a conservatory consisting of three domes, each featuring a different climate, and plants, flowers, and trees that naturally grow in that climate. Each of the three domes is 87 feet high and 140 feet in diameter, with surfaces of glass and aluminum. Support is provided by a framework of precast concrete ribs.

97. Casimir Pulaski High School
2500 West Oklahoma Avenue
Guy E. Wiley, Milwaukee   1939

Casimir Pulaski High School is a wonderful example of an Art Deco education building. The exterior is brown brick trimmed with limestone. A four-story central pavilion is decorated with zigzags, chevrons, and foliate patterns. Students pass through stone-walled entrances carved with historical and allegorical figures and symbols espousing virtue, determination, and knowledge. Low relief sculptures of Washington, Franklin, and Pulaski, as well as the images of Peace (a figure grasping an olive branch) and Strength (a figure holding a lightning bolt) are meant to inspire students. East and west entrances fronting on Oklahoma Avenue exhibit carvings of an Indian chief, a pioneer, a patriot, and a mother holding her child.

Even the doors are significant works of art. Contained in metal window screens are symbolic images of an oil lamp (knowledge), the winged foot of Mercury (Roman god of commerce and thrift), an hour glass in front of an ink well and feather pens (time and knowledge), and a globe (travel broadens knowledge).

Inside the main entrance past the outer lobby is the flamboyant inner lobby with its high ceiling, geometric-design terrazzo floor, and terra-cotta wainscotted walls. Above are stunning eight-sided Art Deco light fixtures.

Pulaski's first class graduated in June 1939. Currently, it has an enrollment of 1,700.

98. St. Sava Serbian Orthodox Cathedral
3201 South Fifty-first Street
Camburas & Theodore, Chicago
Lefebvre & Wiggins, Milwaukee   1958

St. Sava is the largest and most remarkable of its denomination in the city. Its style derives from classical Byzantine buildings of the Serbian Orthodox manner. The cathedral is a cruciform plan, complying with traditional orthodox tenets. From the west portico doors to the apse on the east, it measures 135 feet; transepts are 60 feet across. The congregation of 500 faces east toward the altar. From the cathedral floor to the apex of the central dome is 76 feet. The interior is profusely decorated with statuary, mosaics, paintings, and imported stained-glass windows.

The exterior is faced with limestone ashlar and the roof is topped with five copper domes, each surmounted with a gold-leaf-covered cross.

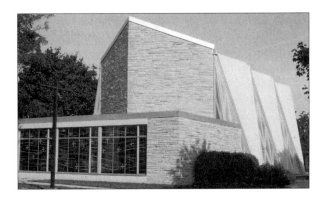

99. Zion United Church of Christ

3301 South Seventy-sixth Street
William P. Wenzler, Milwaukee   1959

Zion is a landmark modernist building whose architect explored alternative ways of designing religious architecture. He reinterpreted traditional needs and arrived at a unique design.

The nave's large stained-glass windows are separated by inverted triangular "sails" of concrete and steel. Each end of the nave is faced with coursed limestone ashlar. An adjacent office and education wing was completed in 1964.

100. Central Steel & Wire Company Distribution Warehouse

4343 South Sixth Street
Friedman, Alschuler & Sincere, Chicago   1956

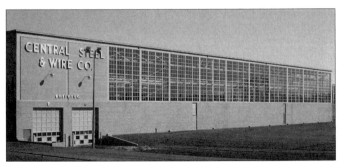

Built with steel, glass, and blond brick, this stunning building owes much of its design to the German Bauhaus. The warehouse is devoid of any ornamentation; it celebrates the utilitarian. This one-story, L-shaped building is 564 feet long and 102 feet wide. At night, its lighted interior is revealed through the thousands of panes of glass that form its walls.

101. Air Traffic Control Tower
Mitchell International Airport
5300 South Howell Avenue
Miller Meier Kenyon Cooper, Milwaukee   1986

This tower rises 290 feet over Mitchell International Airport, making it the tallest such tower in the eight-state Great Lakes region. Four giant concrete legs lift the control room high enough to afford air traffic controllers unobstructed visibility. This tower is a masterpiece of modern design, a sculptural structure that symbolizes flight and the twentieth century with verve and finesse.

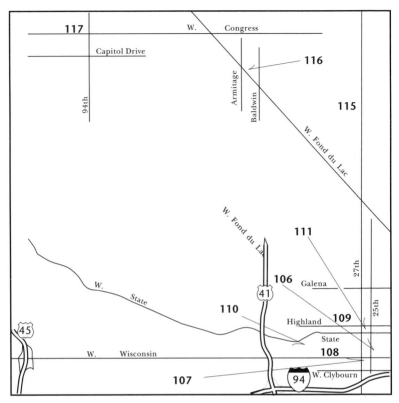

117

W.   Congress

Capitol Drive

116

94th

Armitage

Baldwin

115

W. Fond du Lac

W. Fond du Lac

111

27th

106

Galena

25th

110

Highland

109

W.   State

State

45

108

W.   Wisconsin

41

107

94 W. Clybourn

West and North Sides

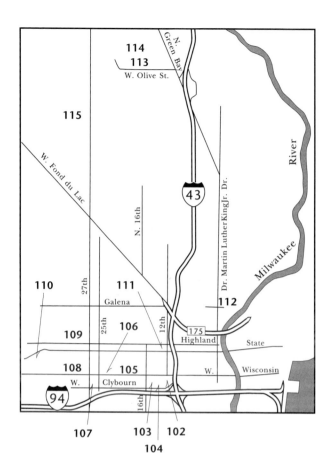

Chapter Four
West and North Sides

The west and north sides of Milwaukee are an urban region of some 50 square miles, home to 370,000 people. Embracing dozens of distinct neighborhoods and ethnic groups, it is home to African-Americans, Jews, Germans, Poles, and others of Asian and European ancestry.

Its architecture spans the time from the Civil War to the present and incorporates every style popular during those years. There are patchworks of Victorian, craftsman vernacular, bungalow, Cape Cod, and ranch houses. Enclaves of brick and stucco Mediterranean style homes, as well as stone-faced "two families," abound. Major avenues are lined with brick and terra-cotta commercial structures of the 1920s. Large parks, manufacturing zones, and retail areas are also found here.

The west and north sides have many handsome neighborhoods that are of special architectural interest. One such neighborhood is Brewer's Hill. This residential and light manufacturing area climbs the incline just north of the old Schlitz Brewery. It is bounded on the west by Martin Luther King Drive, on the east by the Milwaukee River, and on the north by North Avenue. Within these confines are dozens of nineteenth-century homes that have been, or are being restored. These Italianate, Queen Anne, and urban vernacular houses were built by members of Milwaukee's merchant class and by many of the employees of the nearby Schlitz Brewery. This neighborhood is an architectural renovation success story.

Further west, centered on North Sherman Boulevard, is the area known as Sherman Park, with its hundreds of substantial homes spanning the first 40 years of this century. Located here are fine examples of craftsman bungalows, as well as urban vernacular, and even a few Prairie style homes.

West and North Side Buildings

Camel sculpture, entrance to Tripoli Shrine Temple,
3000 West Wisconsin Avenue, 1928.

102. Roman Catholic Church of the Gesu
1145 West Wisconsin Avenue
Henry C. Koch & Co., Milwaukee   1893
Herman J. Esser, Milwaukee   1902

This great stone structure recalls the architecture of Medieval France. Gray limestone walls are decorated with crockets and finials and are punctuated by lancet-arched, stained-glass windows. A prominent rose window fills the center of the church's north facade. Two buttressed bell towers, the tallest rising 180 feet, are surmounted by pointed spires visible for miles.

The church is characteristically cruciform in plan, with a fleche (a small spire) at the crossing of the nave and transepts. The interior is divided into an upper and lower church, each of which seats over 1,000.

The main entrance, added in 1902, consists of three compound-arched doorways surrounded by trefoil designs and pinnacles.

103. St. Joan of Arc Chapel

Marquette University Campus south of the 1400 block of West Wisconsin Avenue
Original architect unknown, early fifteenth century
Ernest Bonnamy of Kahn & Jacobs, New York City   1926
Reconstruction architects, Lucien David, France   1964

Milwaukee's oldest building and one of the oldest in the Western Hemisphere, the St. Joan of Arc Chapel was originally known as the Chapelle de St. Martin de Sayssuel. It stood in the village of Chasse, some twelve miles south of Lyon, France.

In 1926, Gertrude Hill Gavin acquired the chapel. Detailed drawings were made and stone by stone the chapel was dismantled. The stones were marked for proper location and the whole of the structure was moved to Gavin's 50-acre estate at Jericho, Long Island, New York, and rebuilt. Also brought from France were the Gothic altar and the famous Joan of Arc Stone, a niche stone that supported a statue of Our Lady and at which Joan of Arc (1412-1431) prayed, and which allowed the chapel's owners to rename it in her honor.

In 1964, the Long Island estate passed into the hands of others, who dismantled the chapel and donated it to Marquette University for reconstruction. The interior contains ancient banners, torcheres, candlesticks, vestments, a crucifix, a lectern, a twelfth-century font, and the Joan of Arc Stone. Under current French law, it would now be impossible to remove such an historic architectural monument from France.

104. Patrick and Beatrice Haggerty Museum of Art
Marquette University Campus
1300 Block West Clybourn Street
O'Neil Ford, of Ford, Powell & Carson,
San Antonio, Texas
David Kahler, Milwaukee   1984

This is one of the most successful and tastefully designed university art museums in the country. The two-story, 20,000-square-foot museum has a concrete skeleton covered with off-white brick. It is topped with an undulating roof covered with lead sheets. Just below each roof peak are glass channels running the length of the roof that admit sunlight into the galleries below.

105. Sovereign Apartment Building
1810 West Wisconsin Avenue
Bruce Uthus, Milwaukee 1929

The Sovereign Apartment Building is one of Milwaukee's finest examples of an Art Deco residential highrise. It stands eight stories and contains 125 apartments. The exterior is faced with orange brick and trimmed with polychromed terra cotta, marble, and copper.

Centered atop this block-wide structure are two penthouse floors surrounded by terraces. The massing and geometric ornamentation suggest that Mayan or Aztec temple architecture inspired its design.

106. Captain Frederick Pabst Mansion
2000 West Wisconsin Avenue
George Bowman Ferry, Milwaukee 1890

Captain Frederick Pabst (1836-1904), a native of Thuringia, Germany, arrived in Milwaukee in 1848 with his family. As a young man, he became the captain of a Great Lakes steamer and, eventually, part owner of a shipping company. In 1862, he married Maria Best, the daughter of the founder of Milwaukee's Best Brewery. After his father-in-law, Phillip Best, retired in 1864, Pabst became co-manager of the brewery with Emil Schandein (1840-1888), another son-in-law. In 1873, Pabst became president of the company, and in 1889, the firm's name was changed to the Pabst Brewing Company. By 1893, Pabst was America's largest brewer, with a yearly output of over one million barrels.

As their wealth grew, Frederick senior and sons Frederick junior and Gustave each built mansions. The father's home has become the most celebrated. Designed in a Flemish Renaissance style, it has three floors plus attic and contains dozens of rooms. Inside are lavish foyers, hallways, parlors, bedrooms, and a dining room. A huge kitchen, butler's pantry, winter and summer closets, and rooms for the maid and butler fill the rear and top floor. Mahogany, oak, birch, ebony, stained glass, onyx, and marble are used throughout.

Stepped gables frame the symmetrical front facade of tan brick, copper, carved stone, and terra cotta. The roof is covered with red pantile, a type of tile with a curved cross section. The porte-cochere on the west is balanced on the east by a private chapel/conservatory adorned with carved cherubs and human figures, and symbols of the brewing art, including barley ears, hop vines, and beer steins.

Architect Ferry (1851-1918) moved to Milwaukee in

1881 and began practice in partnership with Alfred C. Clas. Ferry won awards for his design of the Wisconsin buildings at the Louisiana Purchase and Pan-American expositions. He was also cited for his contribution to the International Architectural Exhibit at the Paris Exposition.

107. Central United Methodist Church
639 North Twenty-fifth Street
William Wenzler and Associates, Milwaukee 1982

This stunning concrete building is partially "buried" —it is insulated with soil, shrubbery, and meadow grasses. Above the chancel rises a concrete "solar shaft" that serves as a bell tower and houses solar collectors, vents, and light reflectors. Sunlight collected by the solar panels is reflected throughout the building. This is Milwaukee's first solar-heated church.

108. Tripoli Shrine Temple
3000 West Wisconsin Avenue
Clas, Sheperd, and Clas, Milwaukee   1928

This fraternal clubhouse is the city's only interpretation of Islamic architecture. The building is topped by a
large onion-shaped dome and corner minarets. Facades
are embellished with polychromed tiles, orange and
brown brick, and pointed-arch windows. The entrance is
marked by two carved, reclining camels.

109. Frederick Pabst, Jr. Mansion
3112 West Highland Boulevard
Fernekes and Dolliver, Milwaukee   1891

This elaborate mansion, an executive's home during Milwaukee's affluent 1890s, is a fine example of Classic
Revival architecture. An impressive Ionic portico stands in

front of the main block of the house, while a full entablature wraps the building. Quoins anchor the corners, and arched window hoods top first-floor windows. The home is constructed of yellow brick and limestone, and is trimmed with copper detailing.

110. Miller Brewery Stockhouse 1
North Forty-first and West State Streets
LeFebvre-Wiggins and Associates, Milwaukee   1955

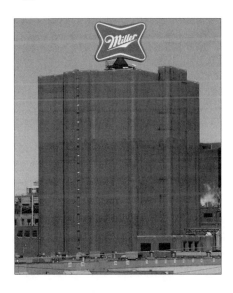

At twelve stories, Miller Brewery Stockhouse 1 is the brewery's tallest building. This Moderne-inspired building was constructed in two stages. Floors one through eight were completed in 1951, and floors nine through twelve in 1955. It rises from a concrete base and is faced with orange brick. The corners are rounded, and facades ripple with brick piers extending from its base to its top.

Stockhouse 1 is an aging and filtration facility housing 240 refrigeration tanks, each holding 1,000 barrels of beer. The building measures 106 by 134 feet and contains over 200,000 square feet of floor space. Above its roof is a revolving Miller sign visible for miles.

111. Sarah Scott Middle School
1017 North Twelfth Street
Herbst Eppstein Keller & Chadek Inc., Milwaukee
Zimmerman Design Group, Milwaukee   1991

This school is designed on a cluster plan. Each of the three clusters houses one grade level, providing a flexible "family" grouping. In this arrangement, the classrooms are placed in groups around a common area. The open classrooms contain movable partitions, allowing teachers to change the size and arrangement of rooms. The school contains 150,000 square feet of space on three floors and has an enrollment of over 600 children in grades six through eight. The exterior reflects interior functions, and resembles a series of small, connected buildings—an "education village."

112. Joseph Schlitz Brewing Company Brew House

234 West Galena Street
Kirchoff & Rose, Milwaukee   1904

Schlitz Brewery was founded in 1849 by restaurant owner and brewer August Krug (1814-1856). In 1858, bookkeeper Joseph Schlitz (1831-1875) married Krug's widow and took over as president.

By the turn of the century Schlitz had become one of the largest breweries in the world. Dozens of buildings, spread over seven acres of land, housed hundreds of employees. The Schlitz Brewery included stock houses, cooper shops, ice houses, brew houses, bottling plants, grain sheds, stables, and office buildings.

In the 1980s, Schlitz ceased operation. Many of the brewery buildings were demolished, but some of the significant structures were renovated into Schlitz Park, an urban office park with its own public school.

A whimsical German Baroque tower rises over the southwest corner of the block-long brew house. The three-story, 185,000-square-foot structure is constructed of Cream City brick on a limestone base. The Brew House is now called the Milwaukee Education Center. It houses 540 middle school students and 900 elementary students. A 15,000-square-foot addition was constructed to the west and is connected to the old brew house by a second-story walkway.

The designers of this building, as well as many other Schlitz structures, were Kirchoff & Rose. Founded in 1894 by Charles Kirchoff and Thomas Rose, it was one of Milwaukee's best-known and prosperous firms. Their work included office, commercial, and residential buildings, all of which drew inspiration from European sources. Herbst Eppstein Keller & Chadek handled both renovation of the brew house and design of the addition.

Terra-cotta horse sculpture, Schlitz Brewery Stables

113. Rufus King High School

1801 West Olive Street
Guy E. Wiley, Milwaukee 1932

Anchoring a neighborhood of handsome 1920s bungalows is the Art Deco Rufus King High School. The exterior is composed of light beige brick, limestone, metal spandrels, and glass, with metal-trimmed casement windows. A central tower rises five floors above the main entrance, which is surrounded by low relief carvings of leaf and floral designs. Symbolism plays an important role here; above the doorway is a female nude (Innocence) holding a lighted torch (Knowledge) while she rests upon a book. Over her shoulder is perched an owl (Wisdom). At the other two Olive Street entrances are carved eagles (Strength) and more owls.

The handsome lobby is trimmed with Art Deco ornamentation: the terrazzo floors with geometric designs, octagonal light fixtures, and a metal screen profusely decorated with foliate designs surrounding the motto *Great Effects Come of Industry and Perseverance.*

114. Emanuel L. Philipp School

4310 North 16th Street
Eschweiler & Eschweiler, Milwaukee   1931

The architects took a decidedly Craftsman approach to the design of this school. Using red brick, terra cotta, handcrafted stone, metal, tile, and stained glass, they created a delightful and practical place for children to learn.

The exterior of the three-story building exhibits extraordinary detailed brickwork. Large panels of glazed orange terra cotta depicting children's storybook characters encircle the building. Stained-glass windows display dancing ballerinas and whimsical figures.

Ledges of carved stone filled with low relief figures, stone menageries of jungle animals, and a few humans lead to the entrance. Above the arched brick entrance a row of large stone penguins seem to greet those who enter.

Inside are terrazzo floors, cream-colored terra-cotta wainscoting, and wood doors and trim. Drinking fountains are recessed into niches where carved squirrels and rabbits look down upon those drinking.

115. A. O. Smith Research Building

3533 North 27th Street
Holabird and Root, Chicago
E. W. Burgess of A. O. Smith Engineering,
Milwaukee   1930

With its undulating glass curtain walls, this seven-story structure is a stunning example of the International style.

The A. O. Smith Research Building was revolutionary in its treatment of facades and the flexibility of interior spaces. Other manufacturing or research buildings were far less experimental in their design; they often had rigid interior spaces and heavy masonry or brick walls with small windows.

The design of this building draws heavily from Germany's Bauhaus, especially architect Walter Gropius (1883-1969). Like its German prototypes, such as the Fagus Shoe-last Factory (Gropius and Meyer, 1911) and the Dessau Bauhaus (Gropius, 1926), the A. O. Smith Research Building is glass-walled and flat-topped, and celebrates modern industrial efficiency. Historicism of any kind was eliminated from this architectural vocabulary. This building predates the completion of the celebrated McGraw-Hill Building (Raymond Hood, 1931) in New York City, generally recognized as the first International style building in America.

116. Capps Drive-In Restaurant
6244 West Fond Du Lac Avenue
C. C. Stark, Milwaukee   1949
F. J. Wilson, Milwaukee   1960

This small building epitomizes the popular culture of post-World War II America. Capps is one of the earliest, and last remaining, examples of drive-in architecture in Milwaukee.

Successfully subscribing to the 1950s "auto culture" design formula, it is centrally placed on its site and is surrounded by paved parking. A thirty-foot, two-legged, neon-encased sign is placed to grab the attention of passing motorists. The restaurant building is its own signboard, a melding of architecture and advertising.

The building has a structural steel skeleton covered with aluminum, glass, painted steel, and ceramic tile. The "drive-in" formula locates a small customer service area up front, with kitchen and storage spaces (enlarged in 1960) in the rear. Customers enter from the sides into an interior of large panes of glass and highly polished stainless steel. Sliding glass windows for order taking are topped by large menu signs. Patriotic red, white, and blue neon and tile walls wrap the building. The drive-in is unique to American culture, and Capps is one of the best examples of this genre.

117. Annunciation Greek Orthodox Church

9400 West Congress Street
Frank Lloyd Wright, Spring Green, Wisconsin   1961

This landmark church, which is actually a few feet outside the city of Milwaukee, is an example of Wright's continual exploration of expressive architectural forms. His career during the 1950s is marked by such noteworthy designs as the Guggenheim Museum and the Marin County Civic Center, a complex that shares many design features with the Annunciation Greek Orthodox Church. An unusual saucer-shaped church, Wright designed it in 1956 and it was completed after his death.

Wright created a modern interpretation of traditional Byzantine forms. A shallow dome is supported by four concrete piers that form a Greek cross in plan. The dome is 106 feet in diameter and rises 45 feet above ground. The church is constructed of reinforced concrete painted a cream color, and is topped by a light-blue, resin-coated roof. Its richly ornamented, circular interior seats nearly 1,000 worshipers on two levels.

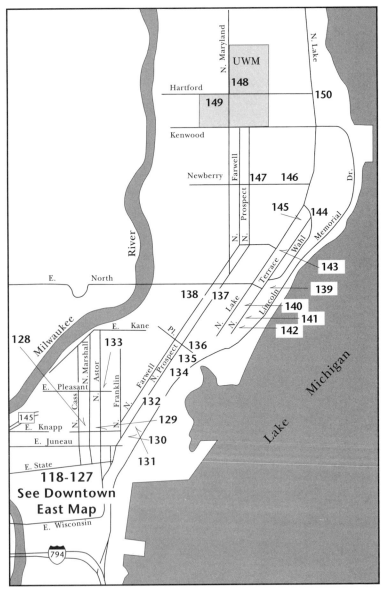

East Side

Chapter Five
East Side

The collection of neighborhoods called the east side is graced by beautiful architectural landmarks, historic parks, and breathtaking views of Lake Michigan. Its front door is a string of lakefront beaches with the city skyline as a backdrop.

The east side has always been a place apart from the rest of the city, culturally, economically, and geographically (it's bounded by the Milwaukee River on the west, Lake Michigan on the east). It is home to three art museums, a major university, schools for the performing arts, and many of the city's artists and writers. Historically, its affluent citizens made the east side the site of most of the city's mansions. It has been *the* fashionable place to reside for over a century.

The east side is brimming with significant architecture. North Prospect Avenue, a busy high-rise corridor, is lined with substantial Art Deco and International style apartment and condominium towers. North Lake Drive and East Newberry Boulevard offer mansions built during Milwaukee's Gilded Age of the 1890s. Fashionable townhouses, row houses, and gracious Victorian homes stand on quiet streets lit by antique lampposts. On the lower east side, small stores and restaurants dot neighborhoods where workers' cottages and wooden duplexes stand side by side. This is surely the city's most cosmopolitan quarter.

East Side Buildings

118 John Dietrich Inbusch House
119 Summerfield United Methodist Church
120 Robert Patrick Fitzgerald House
121 All Saints Episcopal Cathedral Complex
122 James S. Brown Doublehouse
123 Immanuel Presbyterian Church
124 Dr. Henry Button House
125 George P. Miller Mansion
126 Lodgewood Apartment Building
127 Edward Diedrichs House
128 Graham Row
129 St. Paul's Episcopal Church
130 1260 Apartment Building
131 Helfaer Community Service Building
132 1609 North Prospect Apartments
133 Herman W. Buemming House
134 Landmark on the Lake
135 Park Lane Apartments
136 Hathaway Tower
137 Northwestern Hanna Fuel Company Building
138 Oriental Theater
139 North Point Water Tower
140 William Osborn Goodrich Mansion
141 Gustave G. Pabst Mansion
142 Lloyd R. Smith House
143 Frederick C. Bogk House
144 North Point Lighthouse
145 Gustave J. A. Trostel Mansion
146 Benjamin M. Goldberg Mansion
147 Dr. Thomas Robinson Bours House
148 Carl Sandburg Residence Halls
149 School of Architecture and Urban Planning
150 Orrin W. Robertson House

118. John Dietrich Inbusch House

1135 North Cass Street
Leon Alfons Schmidtner, Milwaukee   1874

Inbusch, a German-born wholesale grocer, built this home described locally as "an ornament to the city." The two-story Inbusch house was designed in what was termed at the time a "modern Roman style" and which we know as Italianate. It is built of Cream City brick and rests upon a foundation of sandstone. The design is noteworthy for its harmonious proportions and elaborate wooden cornice, ornamental window hoods, and trim.

The exterior of the house was recently restored. Developers have converted this large single-family residence to a twelve-unit apartment building.

119. Summerfield United Methodist Church

728 East Juneau Avenue
Trumbull & Jones, Chicago   1905

This imposing structure displays a masterful use of hewn, coursed stone. Rough walls of cut sandstone blocks, pierced by limestone-trimmed window and door openings, create a beautiful textured facade. Modeled after the churches of Gothic England, this specimen possesses the characteristic square stone bell tower. This one is 73 feet tall and topped by Gothic pinnacles. Other elements, such as crenelated side entrances, a large rose window, ogee arch trimmings over the doorways, and pinnacled buttresses, contribute to the medieval feel of this distinguished structure.

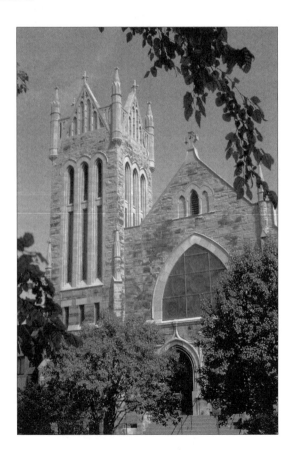

120. Robert Patrick Fitzgerald House
1119 North Marshall Street
Edward Townsend Mix, Milwaukee   1875

This elaborate residence is a remarkable example of Italianate architecture. Built for Irish-born Robert Patrick Fitzgerald (1823-1900), a wealthy shipowner and Great Lakes captain, it was undoubtedly one of the most prestigious homes in the city.

The two-story Fitzgerald House is faced with Cream City brick. Trimmed with a bracketed cornice, the house is topped by a pediment and possesses a handsome Doric portico. As a result of the mass production of architectural components, such wood products as spool finials, soffit panels, rosettes, classical friezes, and whole entablatures could be attached to the house of anyone who could afford them. These items abound on the Fitzgerald House.

121. All Saints Episcopal Cathedral Complex
800 Block East Juneau Avenue
Edward Townsend Mix, Milwaukee 1869
William D. Kimball, Milwaukee 1891
Kirchoff & Rose, Milwaukee 1903

All Saints is America's first Episcopal cathedral, and a noteworthy example of an English Gothic Revival church. Faced with Cream City brick and trimmed with limestone, it has lancet-arched doorways and windows, buttresses, and stained-glass clerestory and side-aisle windows. An eight-sided steeple, sheathed with fish scale shingles and resting on a square bell tower, lifts a cross 190 feet above the street.

Guild Hall, All Saints Episcopal Cathedral Complex

The cathedral, and the Cathedral Institute and Guild Hall, a fine Gothic Revival structure designed by Kimball in 1891, face a commons. Brick buttresses with sandstone caps, terra-cotta hood moldings, trefoil designs, and brick formee crosses contribute to the rich surface texture of these buildings.

Adjacent to the commons is the bishop's house, a three-story Tudor style home designed by Kirchoff & Rose using identical materials and a scale similar to the other complex buildings. On an escutcheon above the porch entrance are carved the symbol of the bishop, a crossed crook and key, and the bishop's hat and cross.

122. James S. Brown Doublehouse

1122 North Astor Street
Architect unknown   1850

The Brown Doublehouse is a rare and excellent example of Federal architecture. Little ornamentation and simple lines characterize this style, which was popular in Milwaukee just before the Civil War.

The two-story doublehouse (adjoining houses sharing a common wall) was built by James Sproat Brown (1824-1878), a lawyer who later became Milwaukee County's prosecuting attorney, state attorney general (1848-1850), Milwaukee's thirteenth mayor (1861-1862), and, eventually, congressman (1863-1865). The exterior is Cream City brick that has recently been stripped of layers of paint. A tasteful interior and exterior renovation has been completed, and today the building is used for retail space.

123. Immanuel Presbyterian Church

1100 North Astor Street
Edward Townsend Mix, Milwaukee   1874

This Victorian Gothic church is a masterpiece in stone. The exterior walls are large blocks of rock-faced white limestone, randomly sized and laid and trimmed with red-orange and gray limestone. Polished granite

columns, wrought-iron grills, and stained-glass windows complete the mix of exterior materials.

Flanking the main entrance are two prominent crenelated towers. The tallest, a buttressed bell tower with lancet windows and quatrefoil tracery, rises 147 feet. A central entrance pavilion with a three-arched portal is guarded by two carved stone, spiny-backed gargoyles. Above are a giant wheel window and a Celtic cross.

124. Dr. Henry Button House
1024 East State Street
Edward Townsend Mix, Milwaukee   1875

Vermont-born Dr. Henry Button (1818-1890), owner of a successful pharmacy and wholesale drug company, built this elegant Italianate residence in one of the city's most fashionable neighborhoods. Exterior materials

consist of Cream City brick trimmed with sandstone, an elaborate wooden cornice, and wood-carved drop finials.

Although Milwaukee has dozens of Italianate houses remaining, this is one of the most prominent and best preserved, in what was once an aristocratic Victorian neighborhood. Today the Button House is home to an art gallery.

125. George P. Miller Mansion

1060 East Juneau Avenue
August Fiedler, Chicago   1885

This splendid three-story structure is one of Milwaukee's best preserved and finest examples of Victorian eclecticism. The exterior, of pink quartzite, brick, terra cotta, and stained glass, is trimmed with sheet copper and elaborate wrought-iron railings. Carved ram heads guard the front porch, while above are a slate roof, copper finials, and decorative chimney pots.

Erected by wealthy Milwaukee department store owner Timothy Appleton Chapman (1824-1892), it was a

wedding gift to his daughter, Laura, and her lawyer husband, George P. Miller.

Isabelle, daughter of George and Laura Miller,
lived in the home until 1980, when, at the age of 91, she
died in the same bed in which she was born. Above the
two prominent second-floor windows are carved the heads
of a young man and woman. One can only surmise that
these are of George and Laura Miller, a fitting remem-
brance of the mansion's first owners. Today the mansion is
used as office space.

126. Lodgewood Apartment Building
1121 North Waverly Place
Fitzhugh Scott, Milwaukee   1954

This was Milwaukee's first International style high-rise residential tower. Sparkling steel and glass walls, underground parking, railing-trimmed top, and flat roof clearly place this design in the 1950s. The clarity and daring of the design echoes other early-1950s masterpieces erected in Manhattan and Chicago.

The 13-story Lodgewood contains 88 units. The tower's saw-tooth north and south facades provide tenants with dramatic views of the city and Lake Michigan.

127. Edward Diedrichs House
1241 North Franklin Place
Mygatt & Schmidtner, Milwaukee   1855

This Palladian villa, an usual design for Milwaukee, has a symmetrical facade graced by a Doric portico, walls with Doric pilasters, and roof-edge acroteria. The exterior of this Cream City brick house is embellished with wood carvings of roses and morning glories, wreath-and-torch designs, and elaborate window moldings.

The interior boasts 14-foot ceilings in the first floor foyer, library, and living and dining rooms. A second floor, added in 1895, was skillfully designed to maintain the integrity of the original facade.

Businessman Edward Diedrichs arrived in Milwaukee from Germany in 1849. Having brought $80,000 with him, he immediately ranked as one of Milwaukee's wealthiest citizens. The villa reportedly cost $20,000, a handsome sum in those days.

Although George W. Mygatt and Leon Alfons Schmidtner are credited with the design of the house, neither drew the plans. That task was given to draftsman Henry C. Koch, who went on to become one of Milwaukee's greatest architects.

128. Graham Row

1501-1507 North Marshall Street
John Graham, Milwaukee 1885

Graham Row is one of Milwaukee's few remaining nineteenth-century row houses. Named for Irish immigrant John Graham, one of Milwaukee's first contractors, it consists of three connected two-story houses. Robust Romanesque forms combine with Queen Anne elements to create a handsome residential block built of Cream City brick and rusticated sandstone and trimmed with terra cotta. Bay windows, arched entryways, and metal finials and weathervanes add charming details. The row, perhaps Graham's largest project, measures 59 feet wide (North Marshall Street) and 61 feet deep (East Lyon Street). Graham Row has recently been redeveloped as condominiums.

129. St. Paul's Episcopal Church

904 East Knapp Street
Edward Townsend Mix, Milwaukee 1890

This massive Richardson Romanesque edifice was constructed of hewn blocks of dark red Lake Superior sandstone, with light brown sandstone window trim. These rugged stones and their masterful placement create an

exquisite tactile surface.

At the southern corners of the cruciform plan are massive Norman-inspired towers, the tallest rising 150 feet. The west bell tower has a stair turret, a common feature of Norman castles. Poised on each of its corners is an angel clutching a copper horn. A wheel window 16 feet in diameter fills the center of the south facade. Other stained-glass windows in the church were designed by the famous Tiffany studios.

St. Paul's is one of Mix's finest works. In this instance, he borrowed freely from Henry Hobson Richardson (1838-1886), one of America's greatest architects, who drew in turn from the medieval architecture of Spain and France.

130. 1260 Apartment Building

1260 North Prospect Avenue
Herbert W. Tullgren, Milwaukee   1938

This great Art Moderne apartment tower, on a bluff overlooking Lake Michigan, is a beautiful blend of technology, form, and 1930s avant-garde styling. The Art Moderne movement was a short-lived, transitional style that flourished during the late 1930s and early 1940s. It closely followed the Art Deco style, borrowing the streamlined forms but eliminating the ornament.

A reinforced concrete structure faced with limestone ashlar panels and steel trim painted dark green, the 1260 Building rises nine stories and contains 34 apartments. There are 32 five-room, two-story units on floors one through eight. Two single-level, six-room penthouses share the ninth floor. The building's elevators stop only on odd-numbered floors, those being the levels with apartment entrances. The even-numbered floors are bedroom levels and are secluded from normal tenant traffic.

131. Helfaer Community Service Building
1360 North Prospect Avenue
Edward Durell Stone, New York City   1973

This modern three-story community center and office building is home to the Milwaukee Jewish Federation and Associated Agencies. Exterior materials on this carefully proportioned and balanced building include ripple-surface concrete and blond brick. Canted walls, embracing large recessed and mirrored windows, create rhythms of shadow and light on the facades.

Inside, a three-story, skylighted atrium dominates the public spaces. Materials employed on the exterior are also used here. On the atrium's north wall is a large tapestry that was specially designed for this space by artist Marc Chagall. In front of the building is a particularly moving Holocaust memorial sculpture, designed by Claire Lieberman.

Edward Durell Stone (1902-1978) is best remembered for such works as New York City's Museum of Modern Art (1939), Washington, D.C.'s Kennedy Center for the Performing Arts (1969), and Chicago's 80-story Amoco Building (1974).

132. 1609 North Prospect Apartments
1609 North Prospect Avenue
Russell Barr Williamson, Milwaukee   1940

A distinguished high-rise noteworthy in the development of Milwaukee's residential architecture, this building rests between the Art Moderne Twelve-Sixty (building #130) and the International style Lodgewood (#126). The 1609 Prospect borrows from the Moderne while anticipating the philosophy of "less is more."

Rising nine floors, the elevations are of sand-colored brick, steel and glass with terra-cotta. The spandrels include Moderne style horizontal ripples. Except for these spandrel panels the facade is unadorned, in typical International style. Compare the Deco appearance of the nearby Park Lane (Stuckert, 1930), erected only a decade earlier.

The 55 apartments offer views of Lake Michigan through metal casement windows. The lobby is lined with glass block and has a floor of polished terrazzo.

133. Herman W. Buemming House

1012 East Pleasant Street
Herman W. Buemming, Milwaukee   1901

This stunning example of Greek Revival architecture was designed by its first owner, architect Herman W. Buemming (1872-1947). The white, two-story frame structure is carefully proportioned. Two-story Ionic columns, acroteria, and a full entablature and pediment make this a noteworthy "temple front" house.

Buemming was an apprentice to Milwaukee architect Charles A. Gombert of Milwaukee and to the famous New York architect George B. Post. As an independent architect in Milwaukee in 1897, Buemming was associated with Chicago architects William Le Baron Jenney and William Mundie during the construction of the Railway Exchange Building (1901).

134. Landmark on the Lake
1660 North Prospect Avenue
Loewenberg & Fitch Architects, Chicago   1991

Landmark on the Lake is among the most fashion-able addresses in the city. This luxury tower rises 27 stories above a one-acre parcel on a bluff overlooking Lake Michigan. Billed as "the tallest residential building in the state," it dominates the east side skyline and offers its residents stunning views of Lake Michigan, the yacht club, and the city. Landmark contains 275 apartments, with penthouse suites as large as 3,300 square feet. Seventy-five percent of its exterior is glass.

135. Park Lane Apartments

1930 North Prospect Avenue
Walter E. Stuckert, Milwaukee   1930

This splendid Art Deco building is nine stories and contains 33 apartments. Completed only four months after the stock market crash of 1929, it embodies the 1920s Jazz Age. Its Prospect Avenue elevation is decorated with zigzags and a host of streamlined forms. Polychrome terra cotta in muted hues embellishes the lower floors. At the roofline, a colorful burst of polished black and gold terracotta trim glows as it catches sunlight.

Architect Stuckert, known as a designer of apartment buildings, teamed with real estate developer Evan P. Helfaer on this and other noteworthy apartment buildings, including the nearby Florentine Manor (1927) and the Embassy (1929).

136. Hathaway Tower
1830 East Kane Place
Herbert W. Tullgren, Milwaukee   1930

This Art Deco condominium tower, nine stories with only one unit per floor, is one of Milwaukee's most glamorous residential buildings. Located on the corner of Summit Avenue and Kane Place (formerly Hathaway Place), overlooking a park and Lake Michigan, it is compact, only 45 by 38 feet. Walls, of glazed blond brick, have rounded corners. Beyond the entrance canopy is a circular lobby with a terrazzo floor, Art Deco dome light, and trim executed in silver and black.

137. Northwestern Hanna Fuel Company Building
2150 North Prospect Avenue
Herbert W. Tullgren, Milwaukee   1934

The two-story Hanna Fuel Building was originally home to a coal supply firm. The exterior is decorated with terra-cotta spandrels depicting the gathering, transporting, and use of coal. Essentially a rectangular brick box, it is embellished with streamlined forms and Art Deco linear brick and terra-cotta designs. Eleven semicircular buttresses, or engaged columns, provide a rhythmic element to an otherwise flat front. Multipane windows span the bays between these orange, terra-cotta-sheathed columns. The symmetrical Prospect Avenue facade has two entrances capped by aluminum canopies, above which are rounded bay windows.

The Hanna Fuel Building expresses the 1930s aesthetic of unbridled industrial growth and human control of "unlimited" energy sources. The company's product is on view; the panels become advertisements for the continued consumption of coal. The Hanna Building is in excellent condition and is currently used as office space.

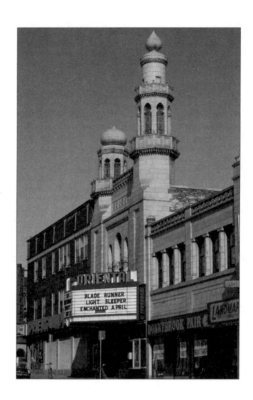

138. Oriental Theater

2230 North Farwell Avenue
Gustav Dick, Milwaukee
Alex Bauer, Milwaukee   1927

The Oriental is one of Milwaukee's last great movie palaces. It originally seated 2,500 in what is described as an "atmospheric house," a theater that was intentionally designed in exotic architectural styles.

The exterior is finished with a veneer of cream-colored stone and terra cotta. Two Turkish-inspired minarets, a lighted marquee, and box office mark the front facade. Nightly, the theater is floodlighted and beacons shine from the windows of the minarets.

Inside, glazed terra-cotta lions, elephant heads, and profuse jewel-like ornamentation surround the visitor in the spectacular lobby. Decorations include Buddhist idols in niches, carved dragons, giant polychromed pillars, and decorative tiles, all illuminated with colored lights. A recent renovation restored the lobby to its original brilliance, while the auditorium was "piggy-backed" into two screens. Fortunately, all lobby and auditorium decoration was restored and is still visible.

139. North Point Water Tower
North Avenue at Terrace Avenue
Charles A. Gombert, Milwaukee   1874

This whimsical Victorian Gothic landmark, on a bluff overlooking Lake Michigan, is faced with limestone and topped by a copper, Gothic-inspired cap with pinnacles. The Water Tower rises 175 feet, 255 feet above the lake level, and was part of a water supply complex at this location. Its purpose was to house an iron standpipe, four

feet in diameter, that would relieve the pressure in the city's water mains. A circular staircase winds around the standpipe, opening onto a small room at the top.

140. William Osborn Goodrich Mansion
2234 North Terrace Avenue
Otto Strack, Milwaukee   1895

The three-story Goodrich Mansion is the finest example of residential German Gothic Revival architecture in the city. It has a symmetrical brick front and sports a lancet-arched portico. Facades are embellished with stained glass windows, terra-cotta trim, and many gables and finials. Two towers, topped with pointed caps, frame this romantic composition.

Industrialist William Osborn Goodrich (1862-1956) was the husband of Marie Pabst, daughter of brewing magnate Captain Frederick Pabst. The designs of both the Goodrich Mansion and the Pabst Theater (1895) were on the drawing boards of architect Strack simultaneously, and he was known as the "Pabst family's architect."

141. Gustave G. Pabst Mansion
2230 North Terrace Avenue
Ferry & Clas, Milwaukee   1906

The Gustave Pabst Mansion is one of Milwaukee's best examples of French Beaux Arts architecture. Built of limestone, it stands a full two stories with a third tucked under its mansard roof. Each of its portico's four Corinthian columns were cut from a single block of stone.

Gustave G. Pabst (1866-1943) was the elder son of brewery baron Captain Frederick Pabst. Gustave joined the business in 1890 and upon his father's death in 1904 he became president of Pabst Brewery, where he served until 1921, when he turned his attention to real estate development and other business ventures.

142. Lloyd R. Smith House
2220 North Terrace Avenue
David Adler, Chicago   1924

This is Milwaukee's premier Mediterranean style villa. In plan, the villa forms a letter U, the open part of which faces west toward the street. An arcaded courtyard with a central fountain echoes Italian prototypes. The house is constructed of white-painted brick trimmed with gray stone, topped by, appropriately, a red clay tile roof.

To the east, overlooking Lake Michigan, are a series of terraces and gardens. Built for an executive of the A. O. Smith Company, it is now Villa Terrace Museum of Decorative Arts.

143. Frederick C. Bogk House

2420 North Terrace Avenue
Frank Lloyd Wright, Spring Green, Wisconsin   1916

The two-story Bogk House is faced with tan brick and trimmed with cream-colored, ornamental cast concrete. Its strong horizontal lines, low-pitched roof, wide

eaves, and leaded-glass windows are typical of Wright's Prairie homes. But with the Bogk House, other design elements emerge. Here, Wright employs a heavy solid look with brick and concrete, and deep-set slit windows. The Bogk is a transitional design recalling Prairie and Japanese themes while anticipating Wright's California houses of the 1920s.

144. North Point Lighthouse
North Terrace and North Wahl Avenues, Lake Park
architect unknown   1912

This landmark was originally located 100 feet east of its present location. The lighthouse was rebuilt inland in the 1870s because of erosion along the lakeshore. Construction was entirely of bolted cast-iron sections, recalling the facade of the Iron Block (see building #28). In 1912, a lower section was constructed of steel plate and the original iron tower was placed on top, resulting in a light that is 160 feet above the lake.

The first lantern burned mineral oil. The present light source is a 25,000-candlepower lamp rotated electrically and controlled by an automatic clock. The lens installed in the original lighthouse in 1868 is still in use. The signal is visible for 25 miles.

145. Gustave J. A. Trostel Mansion

2611 North Terrace Avenue
Adolph Finkler, Milwaukee
Eugene Liebert, Milwaukee   1899

The Trostel mansion, one of the most impressive in the city, contains 28 rooms and over 7,000 square feet. Only the finest materials went into its construction. The exterior is pressed brown brick with limestone trim and large stained-glass windows. The third-floor gable ends are

half-timber with stucco infill. The roof is orange-red clay tile accented with copper finials.

This Germanic home was constructed by Gustave J. A. Trostel, the son of Albert C. Trostel, founder of one of the largest tanneries in the Midwest.

146. Benjamin M. Goldberg Mansion
2727 East Newberry Boulevard
John A. Moller, Milwaukee
George C. Ehlers, Milwaukee   1896

Few mansions can equal the charm of this great house, built by a wealthy attorney during Milwaukee's Gilded Age of the 1890s. This Gothic-inspired "castle" set the standard for other palatial homes.

The mansion is constructed of sand-colored brick

trimmed with limestone and copper. A round turret topped by a pointed spire dominates the northwest corner. Steeply pitched roofs, pointed gables, multiple chimneys, stained-glass windows, crockets, and finials make this one of Milwaukee's more romantic homes. This was the first home erected on fashionable Newberry Boulevard.

147. Dr. Thomas Robinson Bours House
2430 East Newberry Boulevard
Russell Barr Williamson, Milwaukee   1922

The Bours House is one of Milwaukee's finest examples of Prairie style architecture. Roman brick walls rest on a concrete foundation; bands of ribbon windows, unbroken brick piers, and strong horizontal concrete members create a unified design. The clay tile roof is a low-pitched hip with eaves extending well beyond the walls. Through leaded-glass windows, its occupants view a red brick terrace and a "Japanese" garden on the south lawn.

The interior features a large brick fireplace, decorative tile floors, a small reflecting pool, and free-flowing, open floor plan. Its natural oak woodwork remains in pristine condition, as do the original Prairie style sconces.

148. Carl Sandburg Residence Halls
University of Wisconsin - Milwaukee
3400 North Maryland Avenue
Schutte-Mochon Architects, Milwaukee   1971

The University of Wisconsin—Milwaukee campus is surrounded by a well-established, high-density, urban neighborhood. Because of site constraints, the University built upward instead of outward.

The three towers of the Carl Sandburg Residence Halls house more than 2,000 students. The tallest of these, the North Tower, rises 26 floors; the South and West towers rise 20 and 16 floors respectively. Beneath them is parking for some 300 cars.

The design of these dormitory towers was inspired by the post-World War II European movement known as Brutalism. This style was characterized by exposed, rough-textured concrete facades, an emphasis on big colliding forms, and overall monumentality.

These towers, the tallest buildings on campus, provide a counterpoint to older buildings nearby. Just east of the residence halls is the "Quad," a grouping of four Collegiate Gothic buildings. These red brick structures are Merrill Hall (Howland Russel, 1899) and three other halls designed by Alexander C. Eschweiler: Holton (1899), Johnston (1901), and Greene (1904). The juxtaposition of architectural styles, in this case Brutalism and Collegiate Gothic, can be seen as providing visual diversity, or as clashing and unharmonious, depending on your point of view.

149. School of Architecture and Urban Planning University of Wisconsin - Milwaukee
2131 East Hartford Avenue
Holabird & Root, Chicago
Eppstein, Keller & Uhen Inc., Milwaukee   1993

Founded in 1969, the school was located in various buildings on campus until this new building was completed. Four stories containing 150,000 gross square feet, it houses classrooms, design studios, faculty offices, a photography studio, a carpentry shop, a bookstore, and other support spaces. The exterior is composed of concrete and red brick, with window walls of steel and glass, and galvanized metal panels to add texture and interest.

The superbly designed undergraduate studio is 130 feet long and rises 25 feet from gray tile floor to the arched, steel-trussed roof. An immense window wall on the

north illuminates the studio with natural light. On the south wall clerestory windows limit the harsher southern light.

This building is about architecture; in many ways it is self-referential. It has an exposed concrete structure, high-tech light fixtures, visible ductwork and piping, and steel stairways. Handrails are brushed aluminum, a tone that is compatible with the gray, white, silver, and black interior colors. It is a place with clean lines and a rawness not often found in non-industrial buildings. This school building deserves more than just a passing grade; no other building on campus is designed in such a bold and expressive manner.

150. Orrin W. Robertson House

3266 North Lake Drive
Eschweiler & Eschweiler, Milwaukee   1911

Robertson, president of a cement company, purchased this narrow lot overlooking Lake Michigan. Eschweiler's architectural response was to embellish the narrow street facade and to expand the mansion eastward to the lake.

This picturesque home recalls the architecture of

French Renaissance castles and chateaus. The structure is brick and stone with ogee-arched door and window openings. The most romantic aspect of the design is the inclusion of the two feudal-inspired, copper-topped turrets at the corners.

Milwaukee's Fifteen Tallest Buildings

	Floors	*Feet*
Firstar Center	42	601
777 East Wisconsin Avenue		
100 East Wisconsin Building	37	549
100 East Wisconsin Avenue		
Milwaukee Center	29	425
111 East Kilbourn Avenue		
411 East Wisconsin Center	30	385
411 East Wisconsin Avenue		
Landmark on the Lake	27	350
1660 North Prospect Avenue		
Northwestern Mutual Data Center	19	350
818 East Mason Street		
Milwaukee City Hall	9	350
200 East Wells Street		
Wisconsin Telephone Building	19	313
722 North Broadway		
1000 North Water Street Building	24	300
1000 North Water Street		
Bank One Plaza	22	288
111 East Wisconsin Avenue		
Locust Court Apartments	24	280
1350 East Locust Street		
Arlington Court Apartments	24	280
1633 North Arlington Place		
Allen-Bradley Clock Tower	17	280
1201 South Second Street		
Marshall & Ilsley Bank Building	21	277
770 North Water Street		
Regency House Condominiums	27	274
929 North Astor Street		

Bibliography

"Address 411 East Wisconsin" *Milwaukee Journal,* 2 June 1985. Advertising supplement to Wisconsin *Magazine.*

American Institute of Steel Construction. *1967 Architectural Awards of Excellence.* New York: 1967.

Anderson, Harry H., and Frederick I. Olson. *Milwaukee at the Gathering of the Waters.* Tulsa, Okla.: Continental Heritage Press, 1981.

Attwater, Donald. *A Dictionary of Saints.* New York: P. J. Kenedy & Sons, 1958.

Atwood, David, and H. A. Tenney. *Memorial Record of the Fathers of Wisconsin.* Madison, Wis.: David Atwood, 1880.

The Biographical Dictionary and Portrait Gallery of Representative Men of Chicago, Milwaukee and the World's Columbian Exposition. Chicago and New York: American Biographical Pub. Co., 1892.

Bragstad, Todd. "Largest Area Multitenant Office Buildings & Complexes." *Business Journal: Top 25 Book of Lists 1990 to 1991,* 14 Jan. 1991: 87.

———. "Largest Milwaukee-Area Construction Projects under Way." *Business Journal: Top 25 Book of Lists 1990 to 1991,* 24 June 1991: 70.

Brown, H. O., and M. A. W. Brown. *Soldiers' and Citizens' Album of Biographical Record.* Chicago: Grand Army Pub.Co., 1888.

Brown, Martha L., ed. *Developments.* Milwaukee: Department of City Development, August 1982.

———. *Developments.* Milwaukee: Department of City Development, January 1986.

Buck, James S. *Milwaukee under the Charter: From 1854 to 1860 Inclusive.* Milwaukee: Swain & Tate 1886. Vol. 4.

———. *Pioneer History of Milwaukee.* Milwaukee: Milwaukee News Co., 1876.

Builders' and Traders' Exchange of Milwaukee. *Official Directory of the Builders' and Traders' Exchange.* Milwaukee: S. Sarner, 1895-96.

Caspar, C. N. ed. *Milwaukee Picturesque and Descriptive.* Milwaukee: Merchants' and Manufacturers' Ass'n of Milwaukee, 1903.

Celine, Bonny Christina. "A Monument of Faith." *Milwaukee,* July 1983: 24-29.

Coener, Greg, ed. *Developments.* Milwaukee: Department of City Development, October 1978.

Condit, Carl W. *The Chicago School of Architecture.* Chicago: Univ. of Chicago Press, 1964.

Conrad, Howard Louis, ed. *History of Milwaukee County from Its First Settlement to the Year 1895.* Chicago: American Biographical Pub. Co., 1895. Vol. 2.

Coulson, John, ed. *The Saints: A Concise Biographical Dictionary.* New York: Hawthorn Books, 1958.

53 Years on Broadway. Milwaukee: Wisconsin Telephone Co. Public Relations Department, 1930.

First Wisconsin Center. Milwaukee: First Wisconsin National Bank.

Flower, Frank. *History of Milwaukee Wisconsin.* Chicago: Western Historical Co., 1881.

Fried, Joseph P. "Boldness in Steel Design Rewarded." *New York Times,* 27 Aug. 1967: Real Estate, 1.

Gayle, Margot, and Edmund V. Gillon, Jr. *Cast-Iron Architecture in New York.* New York: Dover Pub., 1974.

Gerlach, Frederick. *Frederick Gerlach's Milwaukee.* Milwaukee: The Bookfellows, Friends of the Milwaukee Public Library, 1987.

Germania Building: A Sleeping Landmark Comes Alive! Milwaukee: undated pamphlet.

Gregory, John G. *History of Milwaukee, Wisconsin.* Chicago: S.J. Clarke Pub. Co., 1931.

Kohler, Marie. "Temple of Commerce." *Milwaukee Magazine,* October 1983: 44.

Land, Jno. E. *Milwaukee: Her Trade, Commerce and Industries.* Milwaukee: Jno. E. Land, 1883.

Landscape Research, *Built in Milwaukee: An Architectural View of the City.* Milwaukee: Department of City Development, 1976.

Latus, Mark A., and Mary Ellen Young. *Downtown Milwaukee: Seven Walking Tours of Historic Buildings and Places.* Milwaukee: Milwaukee American Revolution Bicentennial Commission, Milwaukee Landmarks Commission, 1978.

Lehr, Will. "Truly Grand...Terribly Tarnished." *Milwaukee Magazine,* September 1979: 52-57.

Lowe, David. *Lost Chicago*. Boston: Houghton Mifflin Co., 1975.

Milwaukee Chamber of Commerce. *Milwaukee's Leading Industries and Origin, Growth, and Usefulness of the Chamber of Commerce*. New York: Historical Pub. Co., 1886.

Milwaukee Landmarks. Milwaukee: Department of City Development, 1981.

Milwaukee of To-Day: The Cream City of the Lakes. Milwaukee: Phoenix Pub. Co., 1892.

Morgan, Ann Lee, and Colin Naylor. *Contemporary Architects*. Chicago: St. James Press, 1987.

Northwestern Mutual Life Place: A Testimony to Character. Milwaukee: Northwestern Mutual Life Insurance Co., 7 September 1982.

Olesen, Don. "Our Great Indoors." *Milwaukee Journal*, 22 April 1984, *Wisconsin Magazine*: 4-10.

"100 East Wisconsin Avenue." *Milwaukee Journal*, 19 November 1989, Advertising supplement.

Pabst Theater: A Self-Guided Walking Tour. Milwaukee: Pabst Theater Executive Director.

Pagel, Mary Ellen, and Virginia Palmer. *Guides to Historic Milwaukee: Juneautown Walking Tour*. Milwaukee: Univ. of Wis. Extension Division, 1967.

——. *Guides to Historic Milwaukee: Kilbourntown Walking Tour*. Milwaukee: Univ. of Wis. Extension Division, 1967.

——. *Guides to Historic Milwaukee: Walker's Point and South*. Milwaukee: Univ. of Wis. Extension Division, 1967.

Perrin, Richard W.E. *Milwaukee Landmarks*. Milwaukee: Milwaukee Public Museum, 1979.

Pick, John. *Chapel Dedicated to St. Joan of Arc*. Milwaukee: Marquette University, undated pamphlet.

Public Information Committee, City of Milwaukee. *Milwaukee Report 1990-1991*. Milwaukee: 1991.

The River Houses. Milwaukee: Ogden & Company, 1984.

Roth, Leland M. *A Concise History of American Architecture*. New York: Icon Editions, Harper & Row, 1979.

Saint Josaphat Basilica. South Hackensack, N.J.: Custombook, 1969.

St. Sava Cathedral. Milwaukee: undated pamphlet.

Sanderson, Arlene. *Wright Sites: A Guide to Frank Lloyd Wright Public Spaces*. River Forest, Ill.: Frank Lloyd

Wright Building Conservancy, 1991.

"South Side Steeples." *Milwaukee Journal,* 7 April 1985, *Wisconsin Magazine:* 10-15.

Star & Son, Publishers. *1860-61 Directory of the City of Milwaukee.* Milwaukee, 1860.

Storrer, William Allin. *The Architecture of Frank Lloyd Wright: A Complete Catalog.* Cambridge, Mass.: MIT Press, 1987.

Town, Franklin E. *Milwaukee City Directory for 1859-60.* Milwaukee: Jermain & Brightman, 1860.

United States Biographical Dictionary and Portrait Gallery of Eminent and Self-Made Men, Wisconsin Volume. Chicago: American Biographical Pub. Co., 1877.

View from The Tower. Milwaukee: Allen-Bradley Co., Publication 5122, undated pamphlet.

Watrous, Jerome A., ed. *Memoirs of Milwaukee County.* Madison, Wis.: Western Historical Assn., 1909. Vol. 2.

Wells, Robert W. *Yesterday's Milwaukee.* Miami, Fla.: E.A. Seemann Pub., 1976.

Whiffen, Marcus, and Frederick Koeper. *American Architecture: 1860-1976.* Cambridge, Mass.: MIT Press, 1987. Vol. 2.

Whyte, Bertha Kitchell. *Wisconsin Heritage.* Boston: Charles T. Branford Co., 1954.

Willensky, Elliot, and Norval White. *AIA Guide to New York City.* New York: Harcourt Brace Jovanovich, 1988.

William Wenzler and Associates - Architects. Milwaukee: William Wenzler, 1984.

Withey, Henry F., and Elsie Rathburn Withey. *Biographical Dictionary of American Architects (Deceased).* Los Angeles: New Age Pub. Co., 1956.

Woods, Donald A. *UWM Buildings: Some Pertinent Facts.* Milwaukee: U.W.M. Library, Univ. of Wis.-Milwaukee, 1977. 2d ed.

Young, Mary Ellen, and Wayne Attoe. *Places of Worship - Milwaukee.* Milwaukee: Past-Futures, 1977.

Zimmermann, H. Russell. *The Heritage Guidebook Landmarks and Historical Sites in Southeastern Wisconsin.* Milwaukee: Heritage Banks, 1978.

Zukowsky, John, ed. *Chicago Architecture 1872-1922.* Munich: Prestel-Verlag, with The Art Institute of Chicago, 1987.

Glossary

Ashlar—Hewn blocks of square or rectangular stone laid horizontally.

Balustrade—A series of short posts or pillars (called balusters) supporting a railing.

Capital—The decorated top part of a column.

Cartouche—An ornamental panel in the form of a scroll, circle or oval, often bearing an inscription.

Curtain wall—An exterior wall that does not support the weight of the building.

Cornice—An ornamental molding along the top of a building or wall.

Cruciform—Cross-shaped

Entablature—In classical architecture, the upper part of a structure between the top of a column and the roof.

Escutcheon—An ornamental shield-shaped emblem.

Finial—An ornament attached to the peak of an arch or spire.

Gable—The triangular upper portion of a wall at the end of a pitched (sloping) roof. The gable is the part from the eaves up to the point of the roof.

Lancet arch—A narrow pointed arch.

Pediment—A wide, low-pitched gable atop the facade of a building; also used over doors, windows and niches.

Pier—A rectangular or square vertical support which may stand alone or may be part of a wall.

Pilaster—A shallow pier attached to a wall.

Porte cochere—A covered entrance projecting across a driveway through which vehicles can drive.

Portico—A large covered entrance porch, usually supported by columns.

Quatrefoil—A design with four lobes.

Quoin—Large pieces of stone used to accent the corner of a building.

Soffit—The underside of any architectural element, such as an arch, cornice or eave.

Spandrel—A section of wall, often defined as an ornamental panel, between two vertically aligned windows.

Stringcourse—A continuous horizontal band of wood, stone, or brick on the exterior wall of a building.

Terra cotta—A fine-grained ornamental fired clay product used for building decoration, or for art objects such as sculptures. It may be glazed or unglazed, molded or carved.

Trefoil—A design of three lobes, similar to a cloverleaf.

Building Index